# FINANCIAL LITERACY 101

## ——— FOR ———

# COLLEGE STUDENTS

### HOW TO **FIND** THE MONEY,
### **BUDGET** THE MONEY
### & **GROW** THE MONEY

*By*

## CHRIS CORINTHIAN

Financial Literacy 101 for College Students:

How to Find the Money, Budget the Money, and Grow the Money

By Chris Corinthian

1. Business & Economics : Personal Finance – General 2. Business & Economics : Budgeting 3. Business & Economics : E-Commerce – Digital Marketing 4. Study Aids: Financial Aid 5. Business & Economics : Entrepreneurship 6. Business & Economics : Personal Finance – Money Management 7. Business & Economics : Personal Success I. Title. Financial Literacy 101 for College Students: How to Find the Money, Budget the Money, and Grow the Money / by Chris Corinthian

For permission requests, speaking inquiries, and bulk order purchase options, email info@finlituniversity.net

ISBN: 979-8-9869065-0-8

Cover design by Aksaramantra Edited by Brooke-Sidney Harbour

Infinite Growth Publishing, LLC, 13051 Abercorn Street STE B3 #336, Savannah, GA 31419

Printed in the United States of America

# DEDICATION

*This book is dedicated to the dreamers. To those who aspire for greater. To my family...my reason why.*

# TABLE OF CONTENTS

# PREFACE

# Congratulations!

**Y**ou have taken one of the first steps to take control of your finances for college and beyond in, what many call the real world.

If no one has ever told you, I'm telling you right now that "You've got this!" You can and will accomplish everything you've ever *dreamed* of doing. What do you dream of? The mind is so powerful that if you can picture it and believe that you are destined to exceed all your wildest dreams, then you will! In this journey, so many others would have given up on their dreams a long time ago. But you're still here, you're still dreaming, and now you're taking *action* to turn those dreams into reality!

It's not your fault if you never truly understood the first thing about money. Have you ever been confused about your finances? The purpose of money? How to earn it? How it all ties together? Even if you've had money, but never knew how to keep it, budget it, or invest it—it's okay. You'd be surprised at how many people are *still* trying to figure it out. Truth be told, it took most of my adult life of doing all the wrong things before finally learning how to turn this financial literacy boat around.

Do you ever get nervous thinking about the future? If you're somewhat scared about making this transition to college, please know that this is totally normal. It's a whole new world, a whole new lifestyle, another one of life's transitions from one phase to the next. But because you have made the decision to pursue your dreams and go to college to learn more of what you are passionate about, you are showing your courage despite any uncertainty.

Have you ever felt like there's a secret formula that some students know how to keep getting scholarship after scholarship for college, while others can't even get one? Or have you ever felt like there are certain things that people do to grow their wealth over time, while others are still struggling to make ends meet? You know what? You're absolutely right about those suspicions!

Has anyone ever doubted you? Has anyone ever told you that you would never achieve your wild and crazy dreams? They might say things like, "You could never do that, or be more realistic." When you are in the driver's seat of your finances, you take control of your future. By reading this book, you have taken action toward a better life for yourself and your family. Keep taking action and let your success quiet the naysayers!

This book will give you the tools, steps, and resources needed not only to survive, but to thrive!

To get the most out of this book, it's advised to read it in its entirety first. Then, after you've read it one time, you can go back and use it for a reference on specific strategies.

## Who This Book is For

- High school students planning to attend college (especially graduating seniors)
- Current college students (undergraduate or graduate)
- Parents and guardians of high school or college students
- People who want a better understanding on finances and college
- Action-takers
- Goal-oriented people
- People willing to learn
- People whose number one goal is to both graduate college debt-free and have money in the bank

Do any of these sound like you?

## Who This Book is Not For

- People who are not willing to take action
- People who already know everything about money and college
- Complainers
- People who always find an excuse not to take action

If this doesn't describe you, then let's get to it!

# INTRODUCTION

# It's a Different World

It was one of the happiest days of my life! I remember like it was yesterday. On the way home from the hospital, all I could think about was what I had just experienced. My son, Chris Jr., was just born the day before weighing seven pounds, 11 ounces on a very beautiful and sunny St. Patrick's Day in Savannah, Georgia. If you've never experienced a St. Patty's Day in Savannah, just know that thousands of people from all around the city, state, and abroad come to partake in the celebration.

I was on the way home to get some extra clothes and items from our apartment to bring back to the hospital. All the phone calls, texts, and social media posts were flooding in with heartfelt congratulations.

I finally made it home, grabbed the few items to bring to the hospital, and hopped back in the car.

As I was leaving, my phone started to ring. I felt the biggest grin spread across my face as I recognized the name on the screen. It was my supervisor, the director of a large division within the company. As I answered the phone, you could hear my smile on the other end. She said, "Hey Chris, I heard the great news! Congratulations!" I responded with the biggest, "Thank You!" Before I could tell her more about how I was feeling, she quickly said, "Congratulations on your new boy, but we're going to have to let you go." In that very moment, my day went from the greatest I could have ever imagined to the worst day in my life. I felt powerless, confused, fearful, and anxious. How could this have happened? I followed the rules. I went to school, got good grades, got the degree, and finally the great-paying corporate job—all within my 20s. I thought that was the formula for success and security. As long as I showed up on time, exceeded expectations, and was a team player, I would be okay. I was wrong. Unfortunately, sometimes the statements "business is business" and "it's not personal" ring true.

After I got the news, I was frozen in the driver's seat of my car. I felt so stuck. To be honest, I don't even remember how long I stayed pulled over on the side of the road. But I knew my son was waiting for his daddy to come back to him. I then gained enough focus to return to the hospital. During this time, I was clueless on what my next steps would be. Never before had something like this happened to me. Next, I called my mentor, Shed Dawson, and he told me to breathe and that everything was going to be okay. He explained that the Department of Labor had programs geared toward people who run into situations like this. He suggested that I call and make an appointment with them and see what the next steps should be. According to him, these programs help you find jobs to apply for, and eligible people can receive a weekly stipend for a certain length of time. During this time, things were shaky and challenging. But I managed to keep a positive mindset regardless of the circumstances.

A little over two months from the day I lost my job, I started my daily routine for job searching while being a stay-at-home father. What initially felt like a curse turned out to be a blessing in disguise. I was able to spend priceless and memorable moments with my newborn son every single day. Spending time with him each day gave me a sense of hope that things would get better.

One late Friday evening as I reached for the baby's bottle from the warmer, I looked outside and saw my neighbors talking outside our apartment building. This was strange because it was close to midnight, and everyone was pointing and staring at the building. So, I told my wife that I was going outside to see what was going on. I look up to see what they were looking at and found the building going up in flames! Apparently, the fire alarms didn't go off. I ran back in and got everyone out of the apartment. Hours later, we found ourselves looking at the destroyed apartment building.

Soon after, reality started to sink in. You know who didn't want to pay that optional $15 a month for renter's insurance when we signed the apartment lease? That's right, me. No renter's insurance, no job, and our savings were depleted. Sadly, the only money we had to our name was a $250 gift card that the Red Cross gave us to buy clothes from Walmart.

Now, why did I share this part of my story? Isn't this supposed to be a financial literacy book? The reason I shared it with you is because something like this can happen to *anybody*. One day, everything is perfect, life is great, you have your degrees, and you've got job security. Your life is set! But just like that, everything can change. The purpose of this book is to help you become more financially empowered and prepared. Applied knowledge can be a powerful tool when used correctly. That way when *life* happens, and it will happen, you are better prepared for any challenges you may face in the future.

I am so passionate about helping college students get a better grip and understanding of their finances because this is a critical time for you. This is a phase of life when you may be on your own for the very first time. For some, this is an easy transition. For others, this feels nerve-racking and stressful. I totally understand how you could feel at this time.

When I graduated from high school, all I could think about was getting ready to go to college to earn a degree! One of my favorite shows during this time was *A Different World*. I used to watch the episodes and think to myself, "I can't wait to go to a school like that!" I wanted to make my family proud of me for the goals I wanted to accomplish. Fortunately, I had a high enough grade point average that I was eligible for the Georgia HOPE Scholarship, which is a scholarship awarded to Georgia residents who plan on attending a Georgia college or university. I was also one of the Boys & Girls Club of Metro Atlanta Youth of the Year

Scholarship recipients. Due to the two scholarships and a few grants, I was able to start school without having to take out a student loan. Honestly, I didn't know there was a such thing as a student loan.

But after that first year, I found out really quickly what a student loan was. Without going into the whole story, just know that I was considered a "master procrastinator." Have you ever procrastinated on anything? In high school I had no problems staying up all night writing a paper and getting an A on it. There were many instances in which I could cram all night for an exam the next day and get a high grade on the test. Does that sound familiar to you? These habits, I regretfully found out, are not sustainable in college, let alone life. After that first semester, I didn't follow the plan of *work hard, play hard*. But rather I did more play hard, *play harder*. As a result, my grade point average after that first semester was a 1.65. If you don't understand that grading scale, it means I was failing. With grades like that, not only was I at risk of getting kicked out of school, but also of losing all my scholarships.

And yes, I ended up losing all my scholarships after that first year and had to take out student loans the following year. I initially tried to hide it from my mother. But she simply said, "You know you aren't moving back here if they kick you out of school, right?" I didn't know if she was playing or not, but I took what she said as gospel.

Fast forward, and I got nothing but straight A's and a few B's here and there every semester after that. I was able to get my scholarships back and graduated with honors. So, regardless of where you are right now in your college journey, know that it's never too late to turn things around for the better!

During the two years of unemployment after my son was born, I was able to create a few small online businesses that helped me pay the bills. Unfortunately, I had not yet learned how to make them sustainable enough to cover everything each month. Fortunately, I found a job posting for a financial aid position. Because I had experience in this area from working at previous colleges, I applied and got the job. Years later, I became the Financial Literacy Coordinator on campus, where I taught students many of the principles you will learn in this book.

Over the years of working with thousands of students and their parents and guardians, I saw why some students did well with their overall finances and paying for college, and why it was a challenge for others who ended up dropping out because they ran out of funding.

As we travel though these pages on this financial literacy journey, you will see how students like you were able to overcome challenges and have a better outlook on their finances for college and beyond. Your focus is to learn the strategies to earn your degree debt-free, and how to manage and grow your money. So, are you ready to get started?

## The Three-Step Framework: Find, Budget, and Grow the Money

The framework for graduating debt-free from school is what I call the "Debt-Free Degree Triangle." This framework, outlined in this book, is broken down into three parts:

**Section I** – Find the Money

**Section 2** – Budget & Manage the Money

**Section 3** – Grow the Money

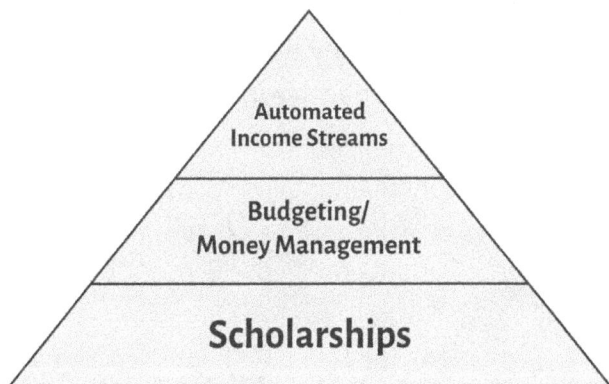

**Debt-Free Degree Triangle**

### Section 1 – Find the Money

In the **Find the Money** section, you'll learn about public, state, and federal money sources such as scholarships, grants, etc. You'll also learn about loans—*and why we won't need these.* Next, we'll go over student jobs, such as work-study and student employment. Then, we will cover tuition assistance opportunities and my favorite—scholarships!

## Section 2 - Budget & Manage the Money

In the **Budget & Manage the Money** section, you'll learn income versus expenses. In other words, what comes in versus what goes out. We will go over priorities and talk about wants versus needs. Next, we will cover money allocation and your daily spending habits. Lastly, we will talk about different tools, apps, and software.

## Section 3 - Grow the Money

In the **Grow the Money** section, you'll learn cashflow principles and how money flows. We'll talk about "The Basics" and fundamentals of money and investing. Last, we will share 15 automated and passive income strategies for college students.

# PART 1

# Find the Money

The reality is that higher education costs money. If you went through public school and thought that college was free, let me be the first to tell you that it can be costly.

Now that we have that out the way, please understand this: wishful thinking does not work. Have you ever tried *wishing* something would just happen without actually doing any of the work?

Let me ask you another question. Wouldn't you feel more comfortable if you knew exactly how much it would cost to attend the school of your choice? Wouldn't you like to know where to find the money to pay for college? Let's start with the foundation.

# CHAPTER 1

# "Free" Money

This section will cover free funding and resource opportunities to help you pay for college.

## *The FREE Application for Federal Student Aid (FAFSA)*

Have you ever heard of the FAFSA? FAFSA stands for the Free Application for Federal Student Aid. You would be surprised at the number of times I have worked with students, and they expected the funds in their account to cover all costs *without* having ever completed the FAFSA. When this happens, some students don't know about the FAFSA, while other students never feel the need to complete one. There are so many types of federal grants that become available to students when completing it.

There are three basic parts to the application process. Keep in mind, it's FREE! (Please beware of the scams that try to charge you to complete a free application.) Here are the three parts:

Part 1: Create a Federal ID

You can go to StudentAid.gov and click on "Create Account."

Part 2: Apply

Go to FAFSA.gov and click on "Start Here" or "Apply."

There are two basic pieces of information that you will need to complete the application. First, basic personal information such as your name, social security number, address, and citizenship information. Secondly, you'll need your household income information for you and your parents or guardians if you're a dependent student. Your dependency status will be discussed in a moment.

Part 3: You'll await a response in the form of an Award Letter from the schools you applied to for next steps. Some schools may need you to submit further documentation if you are selected for verification. This isn't bad if it happens. Verification is the process that colleges use to confirm that the information that you entered on the FAFSA is accurate.

## Message to Parents Starting Early

To the parents reading this book, if you are starting this process to have your child graduate debt-free from college before their upperclassmen years at high school, you may want to consider looking into a 529 College Savings Plan.

A 529 College Savings Plan is a type of investment and savings account where your money can grow tax-free if the withdrawals *(the money coming out of your account)* are for educational expenses. Allowable expenses include room and board, textbooks, and of course, tuition costs. Depending on your state, most of the plans can start with a $25 contribution or less. Currently, the only two states that require more than $25 are Oklahoma and South Dakota, which are over $100 minimum contribution.

## State Applications

The FAFSA is used by many colleges and universities as a universal financial aid application. Be sure to check with your state's application deadlines. Here's an important note: many of the state-issued scholarships have a total amount of attempted credit hours linked to them. In other words, the free state and federal funding resources will not pay for your education forever. There is a cap on how much or how long you can receive the money.

For example, the state of Georgia's HOPE Scholarship has an attempted credit limit of 127 hours. Once you reach 127 attempted credit hours (regardless of how many different schools you attend), you are no longer eligible for HOPE funding. This rule applies even if your grade point average is 3.0, B average, or better.

I'll break down credit hours later so you can get a better understanding.

## *Federal Grants*

There are currently four types of federal grants:

- Federal Pell Grant
- Federal Supplemental Educational Opportunity Grant (FSEOG)
- Iraq and Afghanistan Service Grants
- Teacher Education Assistance for College and Higher Education (TEACH) Grants

### Federal Pell Grant

The current maximum amount of Pell Grant award for the financial aid year in 2022-2023 is $6,895 per year or up to $3,448 per semester.

The federal financial aid year spans July 1st to June 30th of every year. This grant is awarded to undergraduates who display great financial need and do not have their bachelor's, graduate, or professional degree. Also, some post-baccalaureate teaching certification programs may be eligible for the Pell Grant.

Would you like to know how it is calculated?

The calculation is usually based on a few things:

First, it's based on the EFC, which stands for Expected Family Contribution. Your EFC is calculated after you submit your FAFSA. You can search for "EFC Calculator" online to get a rough estimate of what your EFC will be. The other factors include things like household income, family or household size, number of household members in college, etc.

The key formula to better understand how much Pell Grant you may receive is the current Pell Grant maximum award for the year, minus your EFC. This calculation usually tells you up to how much Pell Grant you could be eligible for. For example, if your EFC is zero then your Pell Grant award for the 2022-2023 financial aid year could be $6,895. That's $6,895 minus zero. Or if your EFC is 895, then your Pell Grant could calculate to around $6,000 because $6,895 minus 895 equals $6,000 for the year.

There are other criteria that determine how much you are awarded, such as the cost of attendance (which is determined by the school for your program of study) and if you are full-time or part-time status.

**FSEOG**

The Federal Supplemental Educational Opportunity Grant (FSEOG) is handled by your school's Financial Aid Office. This grant is given to students with the most financial need. Not all schools participate, so you'll want to check with them. The one thing about this grant is that once all the funds have been awarded, that's it. No more money from this grant can be awarded for that aid year.

## Iraq and Afghanistan Service Grants

Here are the current eligibility requirements for these grants:

- You are not eligible for Pell Grant based on EFC. (Remember, the EFC is found at the end of your submitted FAFSA and often your Award Letter, too).
- You meet the other Pell Grant eligibility requirements.
- Your parent or guardian was a member of the United States Armed Forces and died as result of military service in Afghanistan or Iraq after 9/11.
- You were under 24-years-old or enrolled in college at least part-time when your parent or guardian died.
- Equal to the amount of the current maximum Pell Grant award.

## TEACH Grant

The TEACH Grant gives up to $4,000 a year to students who complete courses needed to teach. One of the requirements is that you must agree to complete four years of teaching to receive the grant. If you do not complete that obligation, the grant then turns into a loan. It must be repaid in full with interest.

# CHAPTER 2

# Loans

The overall strategy outlined in this book is to keep you from ever taking out a loan to attend college. However, depending on where you are in your college journey, you may be in a position like I was when I needed to take out some loans until I got my scholarship back. Do you believe it is important to understand how they work? If so, let's break it down.

A **loan** is borrowed money that must be paid back, often with interest.

According to Melanie Hanson with EducationData.org, student loan debt in the US is $1.762 trillion dollars in 2022. Over 43 million borrowers have federal student loan debt. The national student loan debt is a real thing.

Basically, there are two types of loans: federal loans (which are public) and private loans (which are usually credit-based).

This next section can be used as a reference for understanding how student loans work, and how the number of classes taken from one semester to the next can have an effect on your finances. Don't worry if none of it makes sense at first. It took me working in financial aid for a few years before it finally *clicked* for me. As a reminder, read through the material at least once, then you can always come back to the information as a reference. For the most updated information regarding federal student aid, always refer to StudentAid.gov.

## *Federal Loans: Unsubsidized and Subsidized Loans*

Federal Direct Subsidized Student Loans are available to undergrads with a financial need. The amount is determined by your school's Cost of Attendance minus your EFC, and minus other grants and scholarships you receive. "Sub Loans," an unofficial abbreviated name for them, do not accrue interest while you're enrolled at least half-time. The key point here is *while you're enrolled.*

### Unsubsidized Loans

Unsubsidized loans are available to undergraduate and graduate students who hold degrees beyond a bachelor's degree. The interest accrues (or is charged to you) while enrolled in school. You can choose to pay it while in school or defer the payments until you are no longer enrolled at least half-time.

**Part-Time, Half-Time, and Full-Time Explained**

Most higher education institutions are based on the credit system. For example, many majors at a four-year college or university require you to complete between 120 to 150 credit hours to receive your bachelor's degree.

Most courses in those programs of study range between one credit hour on the low end up to six credit hours on the high end—for courses like internships, externships, independent study courses, etc.

On average, most classes are three credit hours.

With that being said, let's take a step back to see how it all comes together:

If most students go to a university on the semester system (fall, spring, and summer semesters), we need to break down how many credits are needed each semester or year. Let's say that you want to free up your summers for vacations, studying abroad, internships, or even working a job. This only leaves you with time to attend the fall and spring semesters each year. Are you with me so far?

Let's say that you are majoring in Basket Weaving. And that four-year degree program requires a total of 120 credit hours.

To begin, 120 credit hours is divided by four years, which equals 30 credit hours per year. Break that down into two semesters (30 divided by 2), and that gives you 15 credit hours per semester. Your semesters won't always fall exactly into 15 credits. Sometimes the order of classes you take may end up being 14 credits in the fall and 16 credits in the spring. If you have 30 hours by the end of each academic year, you're on track to finish in four years.

Now, let's go back to the phrase "enrolled at least half-time." This means that as an undergraduate student, you are enrolled for at least six credit hours. Graduate students, those pursuing their master's degree or higher, need at least four-and-a-half hours to be enrolled half-time.

Here's a full breakdown for undergraduate students:

- Less than half-time means you have between one to five credit hours
- Half-time or part-time is between six to 11 credit hours
- And 12 or more hours is considered full-time.

Keep in mind that to stay on track, you want to attempt an average of 15 credit hours per semester unless you plan on attending the summer semester.

So, why did I take all that time to break down credit hours when we're supposed to be talking about loans? One main reason is that the amount of loans you are eligible for can sometimes be determined by your student classification or how many earned credit hours you have. Another way to look at classification is the grade you're in but on the collegiate level. For example, you are either a freshman, sophomore, junior, senior, or graduate student.

## Loan Amounts

Let's look at the different loan amounts based on your classification:

## Subsidized Loan

You have the Direct Subsidized Loan. This loan's interest is subsidized or "paid for" by the Department of Education while you are in school.

For the Subsidized loan, freshmen are eligible for $3,500 per year, sophomores are eligible for $4,500 per year, and both juniors and seniors are eligible for up to $5,500 per year.

Therefore, a freshman is usually eligible for up to $1,750 in the fall and $1,750 in the spring semester, which totals $3,500.

**Side note:** This calculation/amount does not include the loan origination fees that often have a small percentage. So in this example, the $1,750 loan amount multiplied by one percent equals $17.50 in origination fees (i.e., $1,750 x .01 = $17.50). Next, the origination fees are subtracted from the loan amount (i.e., $1,750 - $17.50 = $1,732.50). The final amount is what's disbursed to you and placed on your student account.

Additionally, loan origination fees may vary from year to year. Please keep this in mind when calculating loans into your college dollars.

## Unsubsidized Loan

Now, for the Unsubsidized loan, undergraduate dependent students are currently eligible for up to $2,000 per year. However, independent students are eligible for up to two different amounts. If you are a freshman or a sophomore, you are eligible for up to $6,000 per year. Juniors and seniors are eligible to borrow up to $7,000 per year. Graduate students are eligible to borrow up to $20,500 per year. Graduate students are students who have earned their bachelor's degree or higher.

## Loan Limits

You may ask, "Can we just take out as many loans as we want forever?" The answer is NO.

Dependent undergraduate students have an overall limit of $31,000 with a subsidized loan limit of $23,000. Independent undergrads have an overall limit of $57,500 with a subsidized loan limit of $23,000 as well. Graduate and professional students have a total limit of $138,500, including undergraduate loans.

## 150% Rule (Sub Loans)

The 150% Rule for Direct Subsidized Loans started in July 2013 by the Department of Education. This rule is pretty simple. It says that your maximum eligibility period (or the amount of time that you can take out a sub loan), is 150% of your program's length. For example, if you are enrolled in a four-year bachelor's degree program, you have up to six years to complete it (and still be able to take out any subsidized loans you're eligible for). To further explain, 150% of four years is equal to six years. Similarly, if you're in a two-year program, you have up to three years.

## Understanding Dependency Status

By now, you're probably wondering how to determine whether or not you are a dependent or independent student. So, before I explain the last two federal loans, it's important to understand the difference between dependent and independent status. Let's look at what the Department of Education classifies as an independent student.

### Independent Student

According to the Department of Education, you are an independent student if you:

- Are 24-years-old (or older).
- Are currently married.
- At the beginning of the school year, you will be working on a master's or doctorate program.
- Currently serving in active duty in the United States Armed Forces for purposes other than training.
- Are a veteran of the United States Armed Forces.
- Have—or will have—children who receive more than half of their support from you between July 1 of this year to June 30 of next year.
- You have dependents (other than your children or spouse) who live with you and receive more than

half of their support from you now through June 30th of next year.

- Since you turned age 13, both of your parents are deceased, you were in foster care, or were a dependent or ward of the court.
- The court in your state of legal residence has determined that you are an emancipated minor or that someone other than parent or stepparent has legal guardianship over you.

## The Parent PLUS Loan

Sometimes, the $5,500 (that's $3,500 in subsidized loan and $2,000 in unsubsidized loans) for freshman dependent students is not enough money to cover their school costs. The parents are often the ones to help the students pay the difference in the total cost. However, they may not have the necessary cash or savings to cover the balance. This is where Direct PLUS Loans or Parent PLUS Loans often come in handy.

A Parent PLUS Loan is a loan available for parents of dependent students. The parent must be the biological or adoptive parent. *Grad PLUS Loans are another type of PLUS Loan available to graduate students.*

The parent borrower is fully responsible for paying the interest and loan amount on this loan. This loan is credit-based, meaning they will do a credit check on the parent, and award based on approval.

The maximum loan amount a parent can take out is the Cost of Attendance minus any other aid.

Let's say the PLUS Loan is not approved for whatever reason. Two things can happen after that:

1. The parent can appeal the denial by getting a co-signer for the loan along with a few other options.
2. The parent can choose to let it stay denied, and the dependent student is now eligible for a higher loan amount.

How does that work? When the Parent PLUS Loan gets denied, the student is now eligible for an increased amount in an unsubsidized loan. Thus, a dependent student can now receive the same amount as an independent student in unsubsidized loans because the Parent PLUS Loan was denied.

Why didn't my loan post? There is something that MUST happen before your federal loans post to your student account.

1. You, as the borrower (or the parent for a Parent PLUS Loan), must complete the Master Promissory Note (MPN) for undergraduates.
2. Many institutions also require that students complete the Student Loan Entrance Counseling.

You can always refer to StudentAid.gov and click on the menu bar to find the link to complete.

## Private Student Loans

Private student loans are different from federal student loans. The major differences are:

- Originate with a bank, online lender, or credit union.
- Need a good credit score or a co-signer with one.
- Need steady income or a co-signer with one.
- Higher interest rates, especially for those that do not consider an applicant's credit.

Like federal loans, many lenders will also allow you to defer or postpone payments on the loan while you are in school. Others may require you to pay an interest-only amount or fixed rate while enrolled.

# CHAPTER 3

# Student Jobs

There are usually two main types of on-campus and off-campus jobs for enrolled college students: Federal Work-Study and Student Employment.

## *Federal Work-Study*

**Work-Study** provides part-time jobs for undergraduate and graduate students who have a financial need. This program enables students to earn money to help pay their educational expenses. Check with your school's Financial Aid Office to determine whether your school participates in the Federal Work-Study Program. Students earn at least the current federal minimum wage.

Your award amount depends on:

- When you apply
- Financial need
- Funding level of your school

## Student Employment

Student Employment, also known as Student Labor at some colleges, is a work program open to all students regardless of financial need. These job positions are usually funded by the individual on-campus departments.

# CHAPTER 4

# Tuition Assistance & Tuition Reimbursement

This chapter covers the different types of college financial assistance that is offered by business organizations and the military.

*Tuition Assistance* is when a company or organization pays for your tuition costs up to a certain amount *after* submitting a bill of your classes and/or course schedule.

*Tuition Reimbursement* is when an organization will reimburse your tuition costs up to a certain amount after meeting certain GPA requirements.

Generally, there are two types of Tuition Assistance programs: Employer and Military.

## *Employer Tuition Assistance & Reimbursement:*

There are nearly 100 well-known companies to date that provide these programs. There are companies like Amazon, Best Buy, Apple, UPS, CarMax, Chipotle, Disney,

FedEx, Gap, and Home Depot. If you currently work for a large corporation or business such as these, contact the human resources department to find out what types of programs may be available to you.

## Military Tuition Assistance & Reimbursement

**Military Tuition Assistance** is a benefit paid to eligible members of the Army, Air Force, Marines, Navy, and Coast Guard. Most branches will pay up to 100% of the course cost. Contact your military base education center and speak with an Education Services Specialist.

The **GI Bill** is another form of military funding for college. This source helps qualified veterans and their family members get money to cover all or some of the costs for college.

# CHAPTER 5

# Scholarships

## What is a scholarship?

Simply put, a scholarship is a payment made to support a student's education. These payments are usually awarded based on academic or personal achievement.

### Fellowship

Sometimes you will hear the term **Fellowship**. This is often in reference to "scholarships" for graduate students in a specific area of study.

## Loans vs. Scholarships

The difference between a loan and a scholarship is that a loan is money you must pay back, and a scholarship is **usually** money that does not have to be paid back.

There are rare instances where a student must agree to complete a specific degree program if they are awarded the scholarship. For example, if a student receives a four-year biology scholarship and they decide to change majors during their junior year of college, that student may have to pay back the scholarship money awarded for those first two years.

There are many scholarships out there that are not program specific. However, there are others with more specific guidelines. The rule of thumb is to know the rules for *ALL* of the money you are awarded.

## *"Show Me The Money!"*

Within the debt-free degree triangle framework, scholarships are the foundation of graduating college debt-free. Scholarships are by far the most leveraged and risk-free way to pay for college. This section will walk you through a proven method that will increase your odds of receiving scholarship money.

This section is broken up into a four-step process:

- The Low-Hanging Fruit
- Have scholarships "Find You" vs. you "Find" scholarships
- Your Five Essential Essays
- The "Two A Day" Method

### The Low-Hanging Fruit

Before we get into the process that my students use to get multiple scholarships, let's start with examining the "Low-Hanging Fruit" for scholarships.

There are five types of scholarships that many students often overlook:

- Local Scholarships
- State Scholarships
- College Choice Scholarships
- No-Essay Scholarships
- Renewal Scholarships

**Local Scholarships**

There are so many instances when I ask students if they looked in their own backyard for scholarships. The answer is usually no. Many of the local resources are often overlooked by students when asked.

**High School Scholarships**

If you are a high school student, find out if your school offers any scholarships to their students.

**Clubs & Organizations**

You may be involved in a school or community organization that offers annual scholarships to their members.

**Religious & Church Scholarships**

If you attend a place of worship, it may offer scholarships to their students attending college.

**Local Businesses**

You may be surprised at how many businesses in your local community would love to offer scholarship dollars to go toward your educational costs. You may consider making an ad booklet that displays their business information for a certain price.

**State Scholarships**

State Scholarships were mentioned earlier. However, there are additional state scholarships to consider. First, check with your state's most popular scholarships. An easy way to find them is to type "State of (Insert Your State) Scholarships" into Google.com. The reason to type it that way is because many states have a "State" university that may pull up that specific college or university (e.g., Georgia State, Tennessee State, Mississippi State, and Florida State).

Many states have minimum requirements to be eligible. Usually, the only two requirements are a minimum Grade Point Average (GPA) and attendance at a public institution within that state.

Another hack is to find state scholarships for your specific major. To do this, simply search online for "State" Scholarships for "Your Major" (for example, "California Scholarships for Film Majors"). This search will allow you to find state scholarships that are specific to your major.

## College Choice Scholarships

The reason I call this "College Choice Scholarships" and place it in the "Low-Hanging Fruit" section is because I found that many students overlook applying to scholarships *at* the college they plan to attend.

The easiest way to find these scholarships is to simply do a search within the university's website. For example, if you go to Savannah State University's website and type "Scholarships" in the search bar, you will find the scholarship application specific to that university.

Another way to find it is by searching the college's financial aid page and looking for the scholarship section. When in doubt, you can always pick up the phone and speak to someone in the financial aid department. Simply ask them if they have any scholarships for students who attend their school?

## No-Essay Scholarships

This is one of the easiest scholarship types you can apply for.

One of my students, Taylor, created a two-minute video for the Taco Bell Live Más Scholarship talking about her passions, interests, and career goals. That two-minute video resulted in Taylor receiving a $10,000 scholarship!

One of the most time-consuming aspects of applying for scholarships is drafting, editing, and finalizing your essays. However, when applying for no-essay scholarships, you can often apply for scholarships within minutes.

If you are a high school student planning on going to college, check out RaiseMe.com. Did you know you could be awarded scholarships for making an A in Algebra or having a leadership role in a sport? For example, CNN covered a story on how Abby Saxastar was able to raise $80,000 in scholarships on RaiseMe.

There's a list of resources at the end of this chapter where you can find many of these no-essay scholarships.

**Renewal Scholarships**

One thing I often find is when students finally get selected as a scholarship recipient, they forget to do one essential activity.

In addition to writing a thank you letter after you have received the scholarship, another important thing to do is renew, or re-apply, for that same scholarship for the following year.

You have already shown that you are a top candidate for that scholarship. So, if the scholarship is not one to auto-renew, re-apply each year that organization offers it.

This previous section showed you ways that you can manually seek out different scholarships to help pay for school. There are ways that you can automate the process to have scholarships that are a better match for you show up in one location for you to apply.

## Have Scholarships Find You: "A Scholly Story"

In the time before the internet, people had to do things like visit the public library and search through scholarship books that were the size of encyclopedias. And encyclopedias are like ALL of Wikipedia printed out and put into stacks of jumbo-sized books.

With the emergence of the internet, there were certain sites that had all types of offers *besides* actual scholarships. They offered everything from loan applications to the next scam that was trying to steal your personal information. Then, when you actually found a scholarship after spending hours searching, it wasn't even a scholarship you were eligible for. Fast forward to today, and things have mostly improved. But you still find so many students struggling to find and receive scholarships.

How do we get scholarships to find us? The easiest way to get scholarships to find you is to use a scholarship portal via online software or an application. One of the apps that I recommend most to my students is "Scholly."

Why Scholly?

Before we go into why this particular app is so effective *for the people who use it properly*, we need to understand *why* it was created in the first place.

It all starts with the founder's story, Christopher Gray. He was the son of a single mother who lost her job during the recession. Things got so bad that there were times when he and his mother were homeless while he was in high school. He decided that going to college was a *necessity* for him. The only problem was that they didn't have the money for him to go to college.

He knew the only way he could attend was either student loans, which he didn't want to do, or getting enough scholarship money to cover his tuition. He often found himself in the public library applying for so many scholarships. When the library was closed, he spent hours writing application essays on his 2008 model smartphone that had a tiny keyboard.

After all the sleepless nights and numerous scholarship applications, his hard work finally paid off. Not only did he receive enough money to pay for his tuition costs, but by the time his last scholarship check came in, he had amassed over $1.3 million in scholarships! That's right, Christopher Gray cracked the code on getting scholarships!

He ended up attending Drexel University and studied Finance and Entrepreneurship. Since Gray successfully found strategic ways to get multiple scholarships, he wanted to make the process easier for others, too. He and two other students came up with the idea of creating an app or software that would match students with available scholarships. Students would simply input their age, demographic information, and interests and Scholly would find potential matches.

Fast forward to his appearance on ABC's *Shark Tank*, and the rest was history. For those who have never heard of *Shark Tank*, it is a business reality TV show where a panel of potential investors (or sharks) listen to entrepreneurs pitch ideas for a business or product they wish to develop and scale. One of the show's producers got wind of Scholly and invited Gray to the show to pitch his idea. On the show, Gray made his pitch to the sharks and won!  Both Lori Greiner and Daymond John made offers to him for Scholly.

Today, the app has over four million subscribers and has helped students win scholarships totaling over $100 million. Gray is focused on creating more of a space and awareness as a social entrepreneur.  Chris Gray's personal philosophy is that "when you lead with the good—confronting issues such as poverty and racism—the money will follow."

Let's get into the keys of making the best use of Scholly.

This three-step process within the **Finding the Money** section can also apply to any scholarship- searching platform. Scholly has all the best features when used correctly.  There is also a list of other scholarship resources that some of my students have found successful. The first step with this (and any other) platform is to create a detailed and current profile.

> **Side note:** Be sure to setup a professional email used specifically for scholarships and school-related things (e.g., firstnamelastname@gmail.com).

Most scholarship platforms look for basic information such as:

- Name
- Gender

- Race
- Date of Birth
- High School
- College (Current or Prospective)
- Major
- Grade Point Average (GPA)
- SAT or ACT scores

Major and GPA are the most important types of information when searching for scholarships. However, this is only scratching the surface when it comes to filling out your profile information. When completing your profile information, the more detailed information you provide them, the better your chances at getting matched to scholarships made just for you.

Filling out your profile completely and with the most detailed information possible makes you eligible for several types of scholarships. Below are the seven main types.

## *The Seven Main Types of Scholarships:*

- Academic
- Athletic
- Ethnic Background
- Religious Background
- Medical Condition
- Clubs & Youth Group
- Unique Talents

I have seen scholarships for students who are left-handed, to students whose parents are Bank of America customers. I have also seen scholarships for vegetarians and for photographers. If you can think of it, there is most likely a scholarship for it. There are even scholarships for people who play video games.

Check off anything that pertains to you directly or indirectly when completing your profile information. It's helpful to understand that there are more than just academic and athletic scholarships available to students.

## The Five Essential Essays

Now that you understand the importance of thoroughly completing your profile, let's get into what I call the "Five Essential Essays" needed when applying for scholarships.

They are called the Five Essential Essays because 99 percent of the scholarship essays are centered on one of these topics or some combination of them. Once you have these essays readily available, it will make applying for scholarships much easier for you.

All you'll have to do is modify a few things to the letter: who the letter is addressed to, the date of the letter, and most importantly, the SPECIFIC things you are asked to address in the essay.

It's important to note that if you leave out just *one* of the required items, you will disqualify yourself from receiving that scholarship.

**Side note**: A great place to store and save your Five Essential Essays and your completed essays are in a cloud-based storage like Google Docs. At a minimum, create two folders: one for your five essential essays and another for your actual submitted essays. Then, you always have access to them from your phone or any computer connected to a Wi-Fi network.

Now that you know the importance of the essays and how to organize them, here are the five Essential Essays (in no specific order):

### Impact Essay

What type of impact do you plan to make after you receive your degree?

### Rags to Riches Essay

What challenges or major obstacles have you overcome? And how will things improve even more once you get your degree?

### Plans for Money Essay

How do you plan to use the scholarship money if chosen? How will this money help you?

### Career Plans

What career plans do you have post-graduation? What will you do once you receive your degree?

**Wild Card Essay**

This essay will vary from year to year. This essay is usually centered around a major current event and its impact on you, your local community, or the world. An example could be, "When Covid-19 was spread throughout the world, how did that impact you, your industry, or the world?"

## *The Two-A-Day Method*

Can you start to see how applying for scholarships can be so much easier when you have a proven strategy? If you have the scholarships finding you and also have your Five Essential Essays, can you see how things begin to get a little easier to do?

Anytime I ask a room or arena full of current college students, "How many of you had to take out some form of student loan?" I usually get the same response. Most of the time 90 percent of students in the room raise their hand. Then I immediately ask a follow up question. I ask them, "How many of you applied for at least 100 scholarships this year?" Most of the time it's not even 10 percent of the room, and that 10 percent is a stretch.

Here's the interesting part. Every single time I ask those students who applied for at least 100 scholarships if they actually *received* scholarships, the answer has always been—yes. I don't even get to the point where I ask them if there were 100 scholarships that they were qualified for.

When I ask these students what their biggest obstacle is when applying for scholarships, they often say they don't know what to write. Now that you have your scholarship platform that finds the matched scholarship applications and brings them to you, and your Five Essential Essays, do you think you could take 20 to 30 minutes of your day to apply for at least two scholarships?

It's a simple copy, paste, and edit now instead of trying to create a totally new letter from scratch for each application. Let's look at that. If you simply apply for two scholarships a day for the next two months, that is 120 scholarships you've now applied for.

To break it down:

- Two scholarships a day over the next 30 days is 60 scholarships.
- Then, the following month, you apply for the same amount for a total of 120 scholarships.

My lucky guess is that *this* is the most scholarships you've ever applied for in that time frame or maybe all together.

Now that you have the blueprint, it's time to put it into action! Here's an example of a student who used this strategy.

One of my students, Bobby, was attending college from another state. Therefore, he had to pay out-of-state tuition costs. He came to me after I spoke to him and a group of students on this strategy for getting scholarships. He told me that he was the first in his family to attend college and that earning his degree was the most important thing to him. He wanted to make his family proud. Yet, there was one major issue. He was now at risk of not having enough funds to cover his overall balance. I told him that he needed to follow the two-a-day strategy in detail and keep working at it until you've applied for at least 120 scholarships.

He took a deep breath, exhaled, and said, "Okay, I'll do it." He told me a few weeks later he hadn't heard anything from anyone. I asked him how many he had applied for so far? He told me 40. I replied with, "You must at least apply for 100." He then told me after applying for 60, "Still nothing." However, after applying for around 70 scholarships, he told me with excitement in his voice, "Mr. C, guess what? I just got a $10,000 scholarship!" He couldn't believe it. Within those few months of applying, he was awarded over $16,000 in scholarships in one semester.

Every semester after that, he kept doing the two-a-day scholarship application process and received more scholarships. Do you think you can take the time to apply for two-a-day, too?

## Scholarship Tips

Here are some things to help build momentum when first starting out. Apply for as many of the no-essay scholarships as possible, especially the ones with an upcoming deadline. Then you can start applying for scholarships immediately.

Apply for as many of these as possible while you are in the process of drafting your Five Essential Essays. This process of drafting and editing your essays should take no longer than five to seven days. Scholly has an artificial intelligence (A.I.)-powered personal writing assistant that instantly proofreads and improves your writing. If you are not using this Scholly feature, you can use tools like Grammarly.

Another way to start building momentum is to do an online search for "Your Major" scholarship + "Current Month" Deadline (e.g., Marine Biology Scholarship March 2022 Deadline).

It's also important to have the "Apply Anyway!" mentality. Even when you're first getting started and there happens to be a scholarship deadline approaching in one to three days, apply for everything listed that you are eligible or qualified for. The essay may not be to your liking yet but apply anyway! In the words of Wayne Gretzky, "You miss 100 percent of shots you don't take."

## Resume Builder

Keep track of all activities that you are involved with, especially extracurricular and service or volunteer activities. On your resume, you'll be able to add the activities you are involved in and list the scholarships you have already been awarded (e.g., 1 in a Million XYZ Scholarship Recipient). This info shows that other scholarship donors and organization are also willing to help fund your education.

## Recommendation Letters

You must have at least two recommendation letters on letterhead. Letterhead is when you have the writer's business or organization's official logo and information somewhere on the letter. Preferably, have one letter from a current or previous teacher, and one from a supervisor if you've already had a job. Bonus: ask for one from a community service organization that you volunteered for. Ask those individuals writing the recommendation letters to type a generic recommendation for you. This will allow you to reuse the letter more than once for multiple scholarships requesting a letter.

## Scholarship Resources

My first recommendation is to use Scholly. The students who I find get the best use of the app are those who finished their Five Essential Essays and did the Two-A-Day Method consistently for at least two months. There is a monthly (or annual) cost to use Scholly. It's definitely worth it when using the strategy mentioned above. The other resources are:

- Bold.org (it has a No-Essay Scholarships section)
- StudentScholarships.org (it has a No-Essay Scholarships section)
- Unigo.com
- Scholarships.com
- ScholarshipOwl.com
- RaiseMe.com (for high school students)

# PART 1 SUMMARY

This section showed you different ways to "Find the Money." You learned about different private, public/state, and federal money (loans, scholarships, grants, etc.). You also learned about the differences between loans and scholarships. Next, you understood the different types of student jobs that colleges offer, such as federal work-study and student employment. Finally, you learned how to have scholarships find you, and how to implement the "Two A Day" scholarship application method.

## *What You're About To Learn Next...*

This next section is also critical in the foundation of your financial literacy as a college student and beyond. We'll be going over the best money management systems through budgeting; in other words, what to do with or how to allocate your money. It's one thing to get the money, but you'll be back to square one with no money if you can't manage your money.

This next section on budgeting and money management will reveal tips and little-known tricks to easily manage your money automatically and systematically.
We'll also finish up this section breaking down credit.

# PART 2

# Budgeting & Managing the Money

This section goes deep into Money 101. What is money? What is the history of money? We're not going to go as deep into the philosophy of money as Adam Smith, "The Father of Modern Economics" and author of a book written in 1776 entitled *The Wealth of Nations* does. But we will go over your money mindset. We'll talk about the importance of understanding your relationship with money. Then, we'll talk about actual money regarding income versus expenses—essentially, what goes in versus what comes out. Next we will go over some key budgeting principles. We'll also discuss how to set up your bank account, wants versus needs, and your priorities. And lastly, we will break down credit, so you know what it is, how to establish and build it, and how it affects you.

# CHAPTER 6

# When I First Met Money

**W**hen I was about five-years-old, I remember my dad driving my friends, Candy and Earl, and me to the nearby convenience store. At first, I was going to stay in the car with them while my dad went into the store to get a few items. But I was a little hungry, so I asked Candy and Earl if they wanted some chips. They did. So, I got up and went into the store right behind my dad. As soon as I walked in, there they were—shiny and bright red bags of Doritos! I swear I heard angels singing when I saw them. I knew my friends and I were about to tear these chips up! So, I grabbed a bag and with a big smile on my face, walked out of the store, chips in hand.

As soon as I got back in the car, we devoured those Doritos so quickly, like it was the first time we'd had a meal in days. Then, my dad got in the car, looked in his rearview mirror, and saw me looking up at him and smiling with nacho cheese Doritos crumbs all over my face. The look on my dad's face *confused* me. I thought he would have been proud of me for sharing with my friends. Let me tell you, if looks could kill, I would *not* have made it past that day.

There were some memorable lessons I had to learn that day. First, my Dad held his composure, and walked me inside to apologize to the store clerk. For what at this point, I wasn't sure. Next, my dad handed me some money to hand to the clerk. We walked out, and before we got back in the car, he let me know that I was in deep trouble with him. He said, "Those things cost money, and you stole them!" It really went in one ear and out the other. I was still stuck on the fact that I was in big trouble. After he dropped off Candy and Earl back home around the corner from our house, we had to have a serious father-son talk to remind me of some simple, but definitely memorable, lessons. Let's just say, my dad wasn't the "timeout" kind of parent.

That was one of my oldest memories of money. That, and every week at church my grandmother would give me a dollar to put into the collection plate during the Children's Offering (which I later found out supported the church's private school). Those were two *very* different memories. Can you remember when your relationship with money first started? What's your oldest memory of when you first met "Money"?

## Money 101

What is money? Merriam-Webster's Dictionary defines money as:

"Something generally accepted as a medium of exchange, a measure of value, or a means of payment."

In other words, a medium of exchange can be, "I'll give you this for that." And value can be that, "We all can agree that this thing is worth this."

To view a short, informational, animated video on the history and evolution of money, go to the YouTube channel *TransferGo* and watch the five-minute video entitled: *The Evolution of Money*.

## Relationship Goals: Your Relationship with Money

Truly understanding your relationship with money is so essential for your financial future. Along with the earliest memories you have with money, your mindset on what it represents and your daily spending habits determine everything.

International Women's Money Coach and Author, Raquel Curtis (also known as "The Boujee Banker") says in her book *Living Boujee & Balanced* that, "Your money mindset is essentially the driving force in your daily interactions with money."

Though she has impacted thousands of women across the globe to find clarity and gain control over their relationship with money, her relationship with money was not always the best.

She said in her own words, "I was spending without regard. Focused on immediate gratification and just trying to enjoy my money because I felt like I worked too hard and deserved to spend it. But short-term gratification wasn't doing anything to the long-term problem I created."

Two of the major ways she recommends on how you can understand your relationship with money is to:

1. Get clear on how having money, or the lack thereof, makes you feel.
2. Understand what decisions or plans you have for the money you receive.

She breaks this down through a series of exercises, including budgeting.

We will get to budgeting in a few, and some tools and resources that will help you automate the entire process.

But first, let us discuss the importance of understanding income versus expenses.

## *Income vs. Expenses*

Before we can break down what our budget is and what a budget truly means, we must understand the money that is coming in (income) *and* the money that is going out (expenses).

We will go more into assets versus liabilities in the last section of the book where we walk through how to setup your Automated Income Stream. But for now, let's go over the basics of setting up where you will place your money once you get it.

The first step is to setup your bank account. You may already have a bank account that your parents or guardian set up for you when you were in middle or high school. If you do, then that's a great starting point.

Another reason I don't want to skip past this step is because you would be surprised at how many college students don't have a bank account and use check-cashing locations so they can cash their work-study checks.

## *Your First Bank Account*

If you do not have a bank account or are trying to open an individual account for the first time, here are the steps and common documents you'll need to set it up.

First, you'll need to choose a bank. You can choose a national bank, a community bank, or a credit union. All have advantages to them, but we'll discuss that later on. Next, have all your documents and items prepared before starting the process.

You'll need the following things:

- A government-issued ID (e.g., driver's license or passport)
- Your social security number
- Your address
- Your initial deposit (i.e., the amount of money put into the account when you open it). Some banks do not require an initial deposit.

Next, you'll want to choose which type of account you will open. I recommend starting with a checking account and a savings next. This is where you will choose one of the products the bank offers. Some of those products include checking accounts, savings accounts, money market accounts, Certificates of Deposits (CDs), and loans to name a few.

Money market accounts and CDs are two types of savings accounts. CDs require you to keep your money in the account for a certain term or period, while money market accounts allow you to access your money without penalty.

Next, you will sign disclosures or consent forms. For your account to be active, you will need to agree that you understand the processes, rules, and protocols regarding your new bank account.

Your final step will be to fund your account. There are several ways you can make a deposit, or put money in, to your account:

- Deposit cash.
- Deposit a personal check written out to you.
- Deposit a money order.
- Set up direct deposit with your employer. Your employer is your on-campus or off-campus job. Check with your human resources or payroll departments. You will need your account number and routing number (the nine-digit code that distinguishes which bank).

- Have someone transfer funds from another bank account.

## Managing Your Account

There are easy ways to get access to and monitor your banking information and activity. The first step is to sign up for online banking and download your bank's mobile app if available. Most national banks have an app available to download to your phone.

You can use your debit card, a bank-issued card that deducts money from your account, for multiple uses:

- Purchases
- Deposits and withdrawals (Note, some ATMs charge fees to use them if they're not your bank's ATM.)
- Transfer money between your accounts
- Balance inquiry (i.e., to view how much money is available to you)
- Keeps you from having to carry cash on you
- You can freeze or disable your card if lost or stolen

Be sure to setup early alerts. These notifications allow you to know when you are getting close to a certain balance in your account. For example, an alert might say something like "Your checking account has reached a balance of $50 or less."

## Retirement Explained

What is retirement? The simple definition is leaving one's job and never having to work again for your income. According to the Social Security Administration, you can start receiving your Social Security retirement benefits as early as age 62. However, you are entitled to full benefits when you reach your full retirement age which is currently 67 for those born after 1960. Why am I placing retirement in this section? A very important account that you will need to open is a retirement account. It's somewhere you can put your money, and it will grow over time.

### Roth IRA Explained

A type of account you can open is a Roth IRA account. IRA stands for Individual Retirement Account. Roth was named after Senator William Roth in the 1990s when the Roth IRA was introduced during the Taxpayer Relief Act of 1997.

What's so significant about the Roth IRA? With Roth IRAs, the money you deposit, known as contributions, and the earnings grow tax-free. Currently, you can contribute up to $6,000 per year to your Roth IRA. You can receive your withdrawals/payouts (or "distributions") from the account during retirement after you turn 59½, tax free.

The difference between the Roth and Traditional is that the Traditional IRAs are generally deducted from your taxable income immediately pre-tax and taxed on the back end. For example, if you earned $40,000 from your job and you contributed $6,000 to your Traditional IRA, you would only be taxed on $34,000 (i.e., $40,000 -$6,000 equals $34,000).

> **Side Note:** This is one strategy to setup your retirement. You can also integrate different strategies outlined in this book to put yourself in a position to be a part of the F.I.R.E. Movement. **FIRE** stands for Financial Independence Retire Early.

How can you open and contribute to your Roth IRA? There are four key steps.

Step 1: Make sure you have earned income coming in. This is usually earned income from a steady paycheck.

Step 2: Choose where you will open your Roth IRA account. Do your research and choose which one is best for you. Some popular brokers include Vanguard, Betterment, and Fidelity.

A simple definition for a broker is the "middleman between you and the investments you want to buy."

Step 3: Complete and submit your application and documents. Documentation may include your social security number, bank information, and employer information.

Step 4: Select the investments that work best for your financial goals. We will cover more on investments in the last section.

# CHAPTER 7

# Budgeting 101

## What is a Budget?

I really like how Tiffany Aliche, "The Budgetnista," breaks down the definition of a budget. She defines a budget as "a physical plan of what your money is doing." Essentially, "what will you do with your money once you get it?"

First, let's go over a couple principles of budgeting. These two principles go hand in hand. They are also easy to grasp and implement once you understand them. Then, we'll go over some simple budgeting methods. First, we'll look at some manual budgeting techniques. Then, we will go over some more simplified and automated ways to budget.

## The Three Piggy Banks Method

The Three Piggy Banks Method of Budgeting was first introduced to me when I read Robert Kiyosaki's *Rich Dad Poor Dad* book. We will give an overview about *Rich Dad's* principles in the last section of this book, and why I believe these principles hold the foundation of business and financial success.

But for now, let's go over the Three Piggy Banks Method also called the "Pay Yourself First" Principle. The reason this is called the "Pay Yourself First" Method is because every time you get paid, you should *first* be putting money toward creating your financial future.

Here's how it works...

When your money comes in, you will take 30%of your income and place into three accounts or "piggy banks." The three accounts are:

1. Savings Account (10%)

This will be used for your emergency fund and long-term savings plans. Your emergency fund is money you have set aside for an emergency or suddenly lose your income. It is recommended to save enough to cover at least six months of your basic needs (living expenses).

2. Investing Account (10%)

If you do not have any specific investments currently, you can simply place this amount into your Roth IRA.

3. Charity or Tithing Account (10%)

As it is said, "Give and ye shall receive." When we freely give to others our time and resources, we will receive the same or more back. There are also many other benefits in doing so.

To demonstrate the principle, if you have a $1,000 check, $100 goes to your savings account, $100 goes to your investment account (or Roth IRA), and $100 goes toward tithing or charity.

## 70/20/10 Principle of Budgeting

Another budgeting method is called the 70/20/10 Principle of Budgeting. This method can be integrated with the Three Piggy Banks Method. With this method, you have three percentages:

70%: Needs and Bills

20%: Savings and Investments

10%: Charity and Tithing

If you want to create a "Play Money" account, you can reduce your needs percentage to 50% from 70%, and have your needs covered by 50% of your income. This reduction will create an available 20% to go toward treating yourself to things you want.

> **Side note**: As you can see, the Three Piggy Banks method can still be integrated with this method. They just combined the savings and investing in that 20% group.

Tiffany Aliche, "The Budgetnista," says you should have four accounts to simplify the budgeting process. You can easily automate this process with your human resources department at your job. Simply, give them the banking information and the percentage of how much money goes to each account. The four accounts are your Bills Account, Spend (or Wants) Account, Personal Savings Account, and your Retirement & Investments Account.

Now that you have your accounts setup, let's go over some simple budgeting methods.

## Simple Methods

### The Envelope Method

First, you will get all your cash from your check that isn't automatically going to your savings or investments. Second, you will get a stack of envelopes. Next, you will write down on the envelopes the different categories that you want to spend on.

Examples of some typical categories include:

- Food
- Shopping
- Gas
- Rent
- Utilities (Electric, Water, Etc.)

Lastly, you will only carry the envelope you need for that day, so you don't overspend.

### The Spreadsheet Method

This is a popular method that many people still use. You simply open a spreadsheet program on your computer (e.g., Microsoft Excel), and type "Budget Template" in the search bar. Once you open it, you can type in how much you earn per pay period and how much you plan to spend in each category listed in the template. The cool thing about this method is you can change the category and the amounts to whatever you choose.

**Side note:** If you don't know how much you usually spend on certain items and categories, open your banking app and look over your bank statements for the last three months to see how much you spend on average each month or pay period.

## Budgeting Apps

Now, let's go over some automated ways of budgeting via apps and software. You can setup the categories within the apps themselves. There are several dozen apps out there that help you budget. I will list a few of the best-reviewed that people use:

### Truebill App

This app's features include budgeting, expense and subscription tracker (e.g., Netflix, Hulu, etc.), and Experian Credit Score Monitor. If you want to obtain all three credit reports through this app, there is a cost associated with it. An additional feature offered by this app is at Bill Negotiation Service.

### Intuit Mint App (and website)

This app's features include budgeting (that can add up to 22 accounts with free version), expense and subscription tracker (e.g., Netflix, Hulu, etc.), and TransUnion Credit Score Monitor. Similar to Truebill, you can obtain all three credit reports for a fee. Another feature of this app is that it also has a Bill Negotiation Service.

**YNAB (You Need A Budget) App**

The key difference with this app compared to the previous two is that it follows a "Zero Based Budgeting" strategy. This means that at the beginning of every month, you will assign every dollar that you have to an account and/or a category.

# CHAPTER 8

# Credit 101

There is NO way we could finish this section without going over credit.

First, we need to understand what credit is and its effect on us. According to Experian Credit Bureau, "credit is the ability to borrow money or access goods or services with the understanding you will pay later."

Let me repeat that. "Credit is the ability to borrow money or access goods or services with the understanding you will pay later." Stated differently, "I will let you borrow $5 if you pay me back later."

## *Credit Score*

A way to keep track of how well you're rated, or how trustworthy you are with borrowing money, is by keeping score. Your credit score is like a report card showing how well you manage your money. Banks and other financial institutions use credit scores to determine if they are willing to lend you (or let you borrow) money. Credit can have an effect on everything!

Credit can affect if you're able to borrow money to buy a car. It can also determine if you are able to rent a place to live when you are living on your own. Your credit score could even be the deciding factor if you get selected for a job or not. Like I said, credit can have an effect on everything!

So, is there a universal way that banks or other financial institutions check or view your credit? The answer is yes. Another name for your credit score is your FICO score. FICO was originally called "Fair, Isaac and Company" and named after Bill Fair and Earl Isaac. It is a data analytics company that focuses on credit scoring services.

Your FICO score is simply a "measure of consumer credit risk." The keyword there is *risk*. Is the risk high or low for someone to let you borrow money (or access goods or services), and get their money back? Most of the time, you *both* agree on repayment terms with a written contract of some sort.

## "The Big Three" - The Credit Bureaus

The next question you probably have is, *who monitors and gives you an actual score?*

There are data collection agencies called **credit bureaus** that gather your account information from different creditors (banks or institutions that lend you money or give you access) and provide a report. Your credit scores come from these reports. The three credit bureaus that collect your personal information and create your reports or credit profiles are Equifax, Experian, and TransUnion.

## The 300-850 Swing

Now that you understand that people are given a credit score, how do you figure out what determines if your score is good or bad? Your credit score ranges from 300 to 850 points. Each credit bureau may have the same or different scores based on the information they collect. Most of the time, they are close in range. The range of a good or bad score varies slightly. However, most banks and financial institutions agree that the lower the number, the more of a credit risk you are.

Usually, a score between 300-550 is considered "Very Poor." And a score between 550-650 is "Poor." A 650-700 score is considered "Fair." Interestingly, a 680 score is often the minimum for most major credit card approvals. A score between 700-750 is considered "Good." And lastly, a score between 750-850 is considered "Excellent Credit."

With excellent credit, you will be offered some of the best and lowest interest rates compared to those with poor credit who have the highest interest rates.

**Side note:** An **Interest Rate** is the amount the lender charges you—the percentage of the amount borrowed, which is called principal. For example, 10% interest on $100 is $10. For a basic explanation, if you borrowed $100 with a 10% interest rate, you would pay back $110.

## My Credit Journey

My introduction to credit and my only lesson on credit was found in getting my first credit card my freshman year of college as I walked through the student center. On that particular day, there were local vendors and businesses selling services and products to the new and current students.

One company offered credit cards to students even if they have bad credit or no credit at all. They said, "Since you're 18 you can apply and get approved for a credit card right away if everything checks out." I applied, and guess what? I got approved. I never had a credit card before. And I didn't understand anything about credit at that point. So, I asked the salesman working with me that day, "How does this credit card work?" He simply told me, "You have a set limit on your card." As I stood there looking confused, he further explained that I had a certain amount of money on that card that I will have credited or access to.

He went on to tell me that I would have access to $300 on this credit card. Now to a broke college kid with no money, $300 was a lot of money! And I didn't have to do anything but fill out an application!

This was too good to be true. I asked him, "What's the catch?" He said, "There is no catch. All you have to do after you purchase something with your new credit card is make the minimum monthly payments. That's it!" From that day on and for years to come that was my only lesson on credit and credit cards.

So, when I wanted to finance or borrow money from a bank for a vehicle, I couldn't understand why I wasn't getting approved and why the interest rates were so high. The simple answer was that my credit score was too low.

How did this happen?

Well, for starters, that initial credit card I got my freshman year was maxed out. This means I spent the full $300 on the credit card and missed making some of those *minimum monthly payments*. I knew I missed a few payments, but I didn't understand why my credit score would never get higher than 525.

*35-30-15-10-10*

This next section is going to break down the biggest factors to pay attention to regarding your credit score. There is a specific reason why this section is called "35-30-15-10-10." These numbers represent percentages of what your credit score consists of. Once you understand the percentages and the points associated with these percentages, you will be way ahead in the credit game.

As I mentioned before, your credit score ranges between 300-850 points. That's a total of 550 points within that range. Before we get into the points, let's look at how the percentages breakdown in your credit score:

**Payment History: 35%**

Are you making all your payments on time? This is the biggest portion of your credit score. This category includes past due items and how long they have been past due. For example, your credit report will show if something is 30 Days Late, 60 Days Late, or 90 Days Late. The longer you take to pay something that is past due, the worse it will affect your score.

**Credit Utilization: 30%**

An easy way to think about this category is how much credit is available to you, and how much of it have you used? Let's say you have two credit cards, and each of them have a limit of $500 each. In this example, you would have an overall limit of $1,000 ($500 x 2 cards).

If you max out or spend all the money on one of those credit cards without using the other one, you have now used 50% of your available credit. But what if you contacted the credit card company of the card that you have not used yet, and told them you want to close it because you're not using it?

If they close it, you are now down to one maxed out credit card. Now, your utilization just went from 50% to 100% instantly. A 100% utilization score is considered a credit risk to creditors.

**Length of Credit History: 15%**

This percentage asks how long you have been using credit. The longer you have been using credit, the more confident creditors will feel about lending you money. Banks typically will lend larger amounts of money to those who have a track record of paying back over years versus someone who just started establishing credit months ago.

**Credit Mix: 10%**

Credit Mix is also known as "Types of Credit." The reason I like the term "Credit Mix" is because the name helps me remember what this percentage covers. The Credit Mix refers to the mix or different types of credit that you have. The two categories of credit are Revolving Credit and Installment Loans.

The main difference to help you remember the two credit types are:

Revolving Credit is credit that fluctuates or varies from month to month based on your purchases with that credit. Typically, revolving credit uses credit cards and lines of credit.

> **Side note:** A line of credit is credit that has a set borrowing limit, mostly from a bank or credit union, that can be accessed by you at any time. A credit union is another type of financial institution.

Installment Loans: Installment loans have a predetermined length to pay it off. They usually have a set price that is broken up for a specific number of monthly payments.

The most common type of installment loans are mortgages (i.e., a loan to buy a home or other real estate), auto loans, personal loans, and student loans.

Also, the payment schedule for an installment loan is also called the **Amortization Schedule.**

**New Credit: 10%**

How much of your available credit is new? This percentage looks at the number of new accounts, also known as tradelines. It also considers how many times you recently asked for credit.

Now that you understand how the percentages breakdown, let's examine how those percentages are looked at in points.

**The Credit Points System**

The first time I heard the **points system** explained was by José Rodriguez, who is known as @TheCreditDude on Instagram, in an interview he did on one of my favorite podcast networks, *Earn Your Leisure* on the *Inside the Vault with Ash Cash* show. He explained that when you understand how many points each category covers, you'll pay more attention to those areas. José went on to say that your score is a range of 550 points (i.e., 300–850). When you convert the percentages into points, it changes the game!

Let's start with the highest percentage, which is your **Payment History** at 35%. To illustrate, 35% of 550 is 192.5 points.

Take another close look. That's almost 200 points of your credit score just on payment history alone! Thus, in this example, you could potentially bring your perfect 850 score down to 657.5 simply by not making on-time payments alone.

Next, we have **Credit Utilization** at 30%. This percentage equals 165 points of your credit score. To keep your score in excellent shape in this category, you will want to bring your utilization to 1-3% utilization. Any utilization over 30% is when your credit score starts to drop much more in this category.

For example, if you have a $100 credit card, you will want to bring your balance down to $1-$3 before the billing or closing date on your credit card statement.

Here is a quick tip. If you pay that left over $1-$3 two days after your billing date, which is not your due date, you will pay your balance down to zero and not accrue any interest from month to month.

With **Payment History** and **Credit Utilization** alone, that makes up for just over 350 points of your credit score.

Before I learned how the points and percentages made up my credit score, my score could never get over 600. I was maxed out on my $300 credit card at the time, and occasionally made a late payment here and there. Even though I was making the minimum monthly payments on my credit card, my utilization was over 90% and my payment history was not in great shape.

With just these two factors alone, your credit score could potentially hover around 500 if you're not intentional about being diligent.

**Length of Credit History** is 15%. This percentage is responsible for 82.5 points. Establishing credit for at least two years is the first mark you want to reach in this category. The next checkpoint is five years, and then anything over seven years is excellent for credit history.

Keep in mind that your credit history is an average of all your credit accounts. Let's say you have one credit card that you've had for five years, and you just got a new one. Then your average credit history would be 2½ years in this example.

When you have different types of credit, the credit history may fluctuate. But generally, this is how you can determine your credit history.

Next, **Credit Mix** is 10% or 55 points. If you have a good mixture of revolving credit and installment loans, you will score well in this area.

For example, in the long run you could eventually have a good mix of credit cards, a line of credit, mortgage, and auto loan.

**New Credit** is 10% or 55 points. When new credit accounts appear on your credit report, you have what are called *hard inquiries* and *soft inquiries* (also known as hard pulls and soft pulls). You will want to have between no more than two to five hard inquiries on your credit profile within a two-year period.

Inquiries occur when banks, creditors, and other financial institutions pull or access your personal information and credit profile.

**Soft pulls** don't count against your credit score. This is typically when you get approved for customer or member accounts for businesses, etc. Your information will sometimes get a soft pull when financial institutions are trying to determine if you would be eligible for one of their products (i.e., credit cards) based on basic information about you.

**Hard inquiries** happen only with your permission, and typically when you are applying for specific types of credit. For example, it occurs when you are applying for a credit card or loan.

Now that you have a good foundation regarding credit, you will know what to look out for.

Before we go to the next section, let me explain how you can establish and build your credit profile.

## How to Build Credit

A popular and safe way that you can build credit for yourself is by applying for a **secured credit card**. Secured credit is credit that is extended to you typically based on money that you have "backed" or guaranteed the credit with.

For example, you could go to your bank (or research different secured cards online) and ask to apply for a secured credit card. I would suggest asking for a smaller amount such as $200. Usually, the bank will have you deposit $200 cash into an account as a safeguard and extend you $200 worth of credit.

The banks are willing to do this because if by any chance you cannot make the monthly payment, they will deduct money from that secured account to make the card payment.

*How to Instantly Establish Credit*

Another way you can instantly establish credit is by becoming an "AU" or authorized user on a parent or guardian's credit card. This works well because you usually will not get the card nor access to the card but will reap the benefits of establishing credit earlier rather than later.

You will not have access to your parent's account information nor be able to spend anything on that card. You are simply added as an authorized user. If your parents or guardians have a great credit profile and have followed the steps above, being an authorized user could help you cover different categories on your credit profile. Many financial institutions don't have an age restriction on authorized users. And the ones that do can add them around 13 to 15-years-old.

Let's say your parent has a $500 credit card that they've had for 10 years and has a $5 balance that's paid on time every month. This account information will now show up on your credit report with great utilization, payment history, and length of credit.

Now that you understand the basics of the credit game, you are leaps and bounds more financially literate than so many others!

**Recap of Budget the Money**

In the Money 101 section, you learned that it is very important to understand your money mindset, your relationship with money, and how you feel about money. You learned income versus expenses and budgeting strategies you can implement. You also learned how to setup your bank account, and the basics of understanding and building credit.

# PART 3

# Grow the Money

### *Grow the Money*

**S**o far, we've covered how to find the money to pay for college, mostly through grants and scholarships.

Then, we covered how to properly budget and allocate your money once you receive it.

Each section builds upon the other. This last section is mainly focused on how to build **passive income streams** while you are *still* in school.

**Passive income** is money that you earn with little to no effort on your part. Now, before you start thinking that this is easy money or get-rich-quick money, this section is definitely not that.

Most of the time when you see people who receive money from those passive income streams, you are seeing the results of a lot of upfront work to set *systems* in place. More on this later.

My priorities for your degree-seeking college experience are: 1) Gaining the best knowledge and expertise in your field of study; and 2) Networking and building impactful relationships with others (i.e., college peers, faculty, staff, and professional relationships via internships and organizations).

With these two as your focus, you don't need to spend most of your time earning what is called **linear income**. We will go over the differences between liner income vs. passive income in just a moment.

Before we dive into these two methods, we should look at the "Rich Dad Principles of Money" outlined by Robert Kiyosaki.

Also, as an important reminder before you consider applying anything mentioned in this book, seek professional advice, mentoring, and coaching, preferably from someone who has a proven track record in that specific area.

# CHAPTER 9

# Lessons from a *Rich Dad*

In the previous section, we briefly touched on one of *Rich Dad's* principles of money when it comes to budgeting by using his "Three Piggy Banks" system.

*Rich Dad Poor Dad* by Robert Kiyosaki is the personal story of Kiyosaki's lessons on money that he learned as a boy from both his dad (the Poor Dad) and his best friend's dad (the Rich Dad).

He gave them those names because of their views or philosophies on money. His father, Poor Dad, followed all the mainstream rules for achieving success but not necessarily financial success. Although he went to school, made good grades, and later got a high-paying job as Hawaii's Superintendent of Schools, Robert's dad spent most of his later years financially broke.

On the other hand, Kiyosaki's best friend's dad was considered to be his Rich Dad. Even though Rich Dad dropped out of school in the eighth grade, he ended up becoming one of the richest men in Hawaii at the time. Rich Dad, like Poor Dad, also believed in a good education. He just wished schools would focus on financial skills as much as they did on academic skills.

**Side note**: I want to stress the importance of obtaining your degrees and striving for the highest levels of education in your chosen fields.   In addition, financial literacy is *just* as important.  The point above about Rich Dad not finishing the eighth grade is not to say that your education is not important.  But it is to show you that no matter how many challenges or obstacles you face in life, you too can become successful.

## Assets vs. Liabilities

The foundation of what Rich Dad taught Robert and his best friend, Mike, is that there are distinct differences between assets and liabilities.

There are many professional definitions in the accounting world for an **Asset** and **Liability.**  However, here are simple definitions to help you remember:

- An **Asset** is something that puts money *into* your pocket.
- A **Liability** is something that takes money *out* of your pocket.

You will understand the differences better as we go through this section.

## The Four Ways to Earn Money

Before we get into the different strategies for Growing Your Money, we need to understand another one of *Rich Dad's* principles for generating wealth. This is found in what Robert Kiyosaki calls "The Cashflow Quadrant ™." When you read *Rich Dad Poor Dad* for yourself, these concepts and principles will be broken down in much more detail.

For now, you just need to understand that within the Cashflow Quadrant ™, there are four ways to make money or four types of people. The four quadrants are: E, S, B, and I.

To illustrate what this looks like, take a sheet of paper and draw a line right down the middle.

Next, draw a horizontal line from left to right in the middle of the page, thus making a cross. In the top left quadrant, write the letter *E*. In the bottom left quadrant, write the letter *S*. And in the top right quadrant, write the letter *B*. And lastly, in the bottom right quadrant, write the letter *I*.

Essentially, you have two categories: the E's and S's on the left and the B's and the I's on the right. Okay, I bet you're wondering what these letters represent, right? I'll define what they stand for first, then give a couple of examples to help you better understand.

Let's start with the E. The E stands for **Employee.**

An **employee** is someone who works for money. In other words, you have a job. In this category, your time is equal to your money. As an employee, you have a boss or supervisor who dictates what you will get paid, how much work you need to do, and how many hours you will work. Most people gravitate towards this quadrant because they see the consistent paycheck every week, two weeks, or month, as security.

People in this quadrant mostly want *security*. They may often say things like, "I want a safe and secure job with benefits."

**Side note:** Benefits are items that you pay for out of your check each pay period such as: health insurance for medical expenses, dental insurance, vision care, long and short-term disability, and the company's general retirement plan.

One of the biggest problems with this category when it comes to earning money is that it is **linear income**—money that is paid to you based on the hours you work. So, if you are paid $10 per hour and work an eight-hour shift, you will be paid $80 for the time you worked. If you don't work, you won't get paid.

The next quadrant below the employee quadrant is the S. The S stands for **Self-Employed** or Small Business Owner.

In the *Employee* quadrant, you work for a job or system. However, in the *Self-Employed* quadrant, you *are* the job. The main differences between these two quadrants are that you decide when, how long, and what you want to work on.

In this quadrant, *control* and *independence* are often most important. Self-employed are also considered *specialized*. They have no boss because they *are* the boss and the employee, too. They often say things like, "My hourly rate is X," or, "The fee for my time and personal service is X." Sometimes they're called "solopreneurs" because most of the income-producing activities fall on them.

You will often see professions such as doctors, lawyers, landscapers, hair stylists, and makeup artists fall into this quadrant. They can choose the rate at which they want to provide their *personal* service. But if they do not show up to *work* their business, they won't get paid.

Why? Because they *are* the business.

Let's look at the right side of the quadrant starting with the B in the top right. The B stands for **Business Owner** or Big Business.

To review, in the Employee quadrant, you work *for* the system. In the Self-Employed quadrant, you *are* the system.

In the Business Owner quadrant, you *create, own, and control* the system. You create a system by leveraging OPT and OPM. These stand for **Other People's Time** and **Other People's Money** in the form of business grants, business loans or lines of credit from banks, business credit cards, and investors. *Freedom* is usually the most important thing to the Business Owner.

The main difference between the *Self-Employed* and the *Business Owner* is that the business owner has set up a system and placed staff, administrators and/or managers to run that system for them. Therefore, the business can successfully run without the need of the owner's presence or involvement. The Business Owner could take a month-long, year-long, and even five-year long vacation, and when he or she returns their bank account is *more* profitable than when they first left.

The Business Owner should be strong in two important factors: understanding business systems (which we will break down a little later) and leadership through teams and delegation.

The last section in the bottom right quadrant is the *I*, which stands for **Investor.** This quadrant holds freedom as most important, too. The Investor has *money* work for them versus them working for money.

In other words, if you took $1 and put it into a machine and that machine spit out $2 after it finished working for you, how often would you put that $1 into the machine? Over and over again, of course.

Investors will invest in things like stocks, bonds, real estate, and other businesses via financial or silent partnerships, just to name a few. The main focus for them is the ROI or Return On Investment. This is how much profit will be returned to them after they invested.

You can make money in any of the four quadrants. However, the fastest and most leveraged ways are mostly found in the B and I quadrants. They leverage OPT and

OPM to build wealth. Time is the most important commodity to them. They are constantly looking for ways to buy their time back.

The advantage that B's and I's have is they can leverage time. Whereas, with the E's and S's, the more successful you are, the more time you end up dedicating to the system.

Cashflow Quadrant™ examples:

Here's a look at an example of a business from the perspective of each quadrant.

**Employee:**

If you work for a burger stand, the owner says they'll pay you $10 an hour for eight hours a day. No matter how hard you work, and everything extra you do to help the business grow and become more profitable, you're still going to get only $10 an hour for your time.

**Self-Employed**

You get fed up with working all day, every day, and decide you know enough about the business to create your own burger stand. You buy all the materials, get the stand built, buy all the food in bulk to cook, and even charge a little more for your burgers. The only issue is that you are responsible for all the day-to-day tasks and responsibilities now.

Before you were only required to work your eight-hour shift. But now, you find yourself working 10 to 12-hour days just to maintain the increased income and lifestyle you now have.

**Business Owner**

Next, you take the previous business model in the S quadrant and work on putting systems in place with the goal of removing yourself *completely* from the day-to-day operations. You hire a manager to run the business for you, and eventually turn the burger stand into a franchise.

A **franchise** is a business where the owner licenses the operations (i.e., the products, procedures, and branding) in exchange for a franchise fee.

**Investor**

As an investor, you could take the profits from the business and invest in assets that could grow your money in a more passive manner. Examples include investing in stocks and the real estate and land where the business is located.

Some of these concepts and ideas are very similar to what Ray Kroc, the founder of McDonald's, did. Often, when he asked people what business he was in, they would quickly say "the hamburger business!" He would often respond with, "I'm not in the burger business. I'm in the real estate business."

If you ever get the chance, read how McDonald's grew their business and watch the movie inspired by Ray Kroc's story called "The Founder" starring Michael Keaton. You'll see how that empire grew to what it is today.

## Real Estate

While we're on the subject of Real Estate, let's talk about a couple strategies (because there are literally hundreds of ways) of how some investors use real estate as an investment vehicle.

Quick question. Is the house you live in, known as your primary residence, an asset or a liability based on the definitions we mentioned earlier? Remember, an *asset* puts money into your pocket, while a *liability* takes money out of your pocket.

Therefore, the quick answer to that question is—it depends.

If you are paying money out of your pocket each month by paying rent to a **landlord**, which is a person or entity who owns the property and then rents it out to you in exchange for payment, then it is a liability. Even if you own your home in the form of a mortgage, you still must pay the lender. The mortgage is just a fancy word for the agreement between you and the lender or bank. It states that if you don't pay, they have the right to take the property from you.

So, how can you turn the house you live in into an asset?

To answer the question, one way that people turn their home into an asset, by creating income from their primary residence, is by renting out their home or rooms via an online marketplace such as Airbnb. It got its name from **Air** [mattress] **Bed and Breakfast**. People list their houses or rooms on the platform and list the cost for paying guests to sleep there for a set time period.

Another way is by purchasing a multifamily home to live in such as a duplex (or a two-unit), a three-plex, or four-plex that has four units in one building. Four units or less is still considered "residential property." Five or more units are often considered "commercial property." The property that Ray Kroc invested for McDonald's business was considered commercial property.

In the case of four-unit homes, some people decide to live in one unit and rent out the other three as a landlord because their tenants can pay enough rent to cover the entire mortgage. This strategy will allow for a positive cash flow, thus making it an asset and putting money into their pockets after all expenses. Even with collecting the rent, they could pay a property management company to take care of all the business regarding the property.

Lastly, some people want the benefits of investing in income-producing real estate *without* having to deal with any of the day-to-day operations of that business model.

They achieve this goal by investing in **REITs (Real Estate Investment Trusts)**. These are companies that own many types of commercial real estate such as apartment buildings, shopping centers, hotels, and hospitals. You can purchase REITs on the stock market.

There are also groups that are similar to REITs called **REIGs (Real Estate Investment Groups)**. People invest directly on the stock market exchanges or use investment platforms such as Fundrise.com and Groundfloor.com. For those who want more of a hands-off approach to real estate investing, some use platforms like Peer-Street.com.

## Suzie's Journey

Next, I want to help simplify the idea of the Cashflow Quadrant ™ through an easy-to-follow illustration.

This example is one that I've shared with hundreds of high school and college students to help them understand that these principles can be applied to almost any business idea.

So, here it is. Let's say that nine-year-old Suzie is on summer break from school, and each day she goes outside to play with her friends. But one day she notices something different. There's a lemonade stand two houses down from where she lives. She's been playing in the sun all day and decides to go to the lemonade stand for a drink. So, she runs inside and asks her mom if she can have money for a lemonade. After her mom steps outside to see her friend and neighbor standing next to the stand, she decides to give Suzie a few dollars for a drink.

So excited, Suzie gives her mother the biggest hug thanking her for the money to get the lemonade. She sprints down the street to get in line behind two other kids at the stand. By the time she places her order, she is somewhat surprised at what she sees. Instead of an adult, she's greeted by one of her classmates who takes her order. "Michelle??" Suzie yells out. "How are your parents letting you take orders for *their* lemonade stand?" Michelle smiles with a sense of pride, and lets Suzie know that this wasn't her parents' lemonade stand. But it was actually owned and operated *solely* by her. Suzie was shocked. She couldn't believe that Michelle, another nine-year-old like her, was running her own lemonade stand.

When Suzie purchased her $1 lemonade and saw 20 other neighborhood kids in line behind her, it didn't take her long to see that Michelle was bringing in a lot of money, much more than Suzie had ever seen in her entire nine-year-old life!

Suzie asked right there on the spot, "Michelle, can I work for you? I've been wanting to buy a few things before we go back to school and letting me work for you would be a dream come true!" Michelle sat there for a few seconds and told Suzie "You got the job! You can start tomorrow morning at 11:00 if it's okay with your mom. I'll pay you $10 a day working Monday through Friday."

After Suzie ran home to tell her mother the great news, her mother allowed her to work at Michelle's lemonade stand for a few hours a day during the week if she took care of all her house responsibilities first.

Suzie couldn't wait to show up at her new job the very next morning. As soon as she got there, Michelle had a long list of tasks that Suzie needed to complete before they opened for business that day. She had to do things like unpack all the materials, stack the cups, open the packages, place the plastic chairs in the grass for the customers to sit and drink their lemonade, and on and on and on.

After she completed that long list of tasks, they were finally ready to open for business. While she was setting everything up, she could see her friends playing and having fun in the neighborhood. A big part of her wanted to enjoy that play time with her friends. But she knew that to get that $10, she would have to work at her new job.

The day was so busy with a constant flow of customers. Suzie would accept payment and give the kids their lemonade, while Michelle would mix the lemonade right behind her.

After Suzie's first day of working hard, she saw that the business brought in a little over $100 in a day. Suzie couldn't believe it! As she's looking at Michelle counting all the $1 bills, she's looking in anticipation that maybe (just maybe), she might get a lot more money than the $10 she agreed to work for.

But Michelle gave her that "business is business" look and handed Suzie the $10 that they agreed to.

**Side note:** One thing to always remember is never work a job as an employee *just* for the money. Instead, work a job for the knowledge and expertise you'll gain from the experience.

After working there each day for a week, Suzie knew the ins and outs of how Michelle ran her lemonade stand. Although Suzie had all these great ideas about adding additional flavors of lemonade to possibly get more customers or more sales, Michelle didn't want to do any of that.

Because Suzie had these great ideas to sell other flavors that Michelle was not willing to make, she went home and asked her mom if she could assist her with opening her *own* lemonade stand. Her mom looked at her with a smile on her face and said, "I would be happy to help you set up your own stand." Her mother went on to tell her to have a conversation with Michelle thanking her for the opportunity and see if there is anything she needs completed before her last day of work.

After Suzie and her mother went shopping to purchase everything she needed in bulk, she immediately came back home and started prepping everything to start business the next day.

Because she is doing business similar to how Michelle started out, she will be running the lemonade stand by herself as a **sole proprietor**. We'll break down what that term means in more detail a little later.

Suzie is now running her own business and has grown the business to $120 a day. This is after working her business for a couple of weeks. There were some days within those first two weeks in which she didn't make any money. Also, she is making much more money *now*, but there are some differences that she quickly noticed as a **self-employed** business owner.

She noticed that when she was working for Michelle, she would only have to work a few hours each day and get her guaranteed $10. She would even have time to still play with her friends after she was done working for the day.

Now, she must start earlier and end later than when she just had a job. She no longer has time to play with her friends during the day.

One of her cousins named Josh was living with her for the summer. Suzie asked him if he wanted to make some money during the time that he was there. He said he would love to! So, she hired him on the spot to help her with the day-to-day tasks. When he asked her how much he would get paid, she offered him $20. That's double what her *competition* paid her as an **employee**.

From the beginning, Suzie decided to set up systems to make the daily tasks that it took two people to do into one person's job. One of Suzie's friends from the next neighborhood over saw what she was doing and wanted to work for her, too. Instead of having her friend work for her stand, she decided to get a stand built at her friend's house with her parents' permission. Because she had this easy-to-follow system, she was now able to duplicate everything she did for the first one. Suzie's friend was going to be paid at the same daily rate of $20.

This is how Suzie transitioned from the self-employed quadrant into the business owner quadrant. Since she was able to create systems and leverage other people's time and energy, she was then able to take herself completely out of the day-to-day responsibilities.

Before, she had to work at her business all day. Now, she could sit in the house all day for the rest of the summer if she wanted to. And guess what? She's still making a profit. Both of her stands are each bringing in $120 a day. After she pays both of her stand managers $20 each, she is still profiting $100 per stand every day. That's $200 a day or $1,000 a week without having to show up at all.

> **Side note**: For this simplified example, let's just say Suzie's parents sponsored the materials and other business expenses.

Remember when we mentioned the term **sole-proprietor**? That means that Suzie was running a business that had no distinction between her and the business. I'm not saying that this would happen in *this* instance. But, if a dissatisfied customer wanted to sue Suzie because her lemonade did not taste good (or for any other reason), she could be held personally liable. This means her personal assets could be in jeopardy of being seized or used as collateral.

As a result, her mother walked her through the process of setting up a legal structure that would limit her personal liability. The legal structure in this instance is an **LLC (or Limited Liability Company)**. Now, Suzie has a business entity called "Suzie's Sweet Lemon Juice, LLC."

**Suzie's Journey**

Suzie's new legal structure separated her from her business with regard to personal liability. It also allowed her to have some tax benefits that her mother explained to her.

> **Side note:** In this story of Suzie's Journey, her mother is a small business attorney.

When it comes to working as an employee, you are often taxed first and paid with after-tax dollars. As a business owner, there are many opportunities to pay for all the acceptable business expenses first, including your salary, before your business is taxed.

The Internal Revenue Service (IRS) even allows you to apply for what I call your business' "social security number." This number is called your **EIN** or **Employer Identification Number**.

Now, when Suzie is making her business transactions, she keeps everything separate. Instead of the business purchases coming out of a personal account, everything can come out of the business checking account.

She is able to keep a good pulse on how her business is doing overall by understanding her **Financial Statement**. Her financial statement is made up of three parts: **Income Statement** (which shows the income coming in and expenses going out), the **Balance Sheet** (which shows the business's assets and liabilities), and the **Statement of Cashflow** (which shows how and where the money is moving and if it is profitable or not).

> **Side note**: There are apps like QuickBooks that allow you to take pictures of receipts, and store and categorize them to help you keep track of business purchases. This is helpful when it is time to file your taxes.

*Tax* is defined as money that the government requires a person to pay to support the government.

Also, one business income strategy that's very helpful for businesses trying to better manage their money is using the *Profit First* method by Mike Michalowicz. His unique strategy of allocating the business income has helped businesses even survive the pandemic of 2020 and 2021.

When setting up a business checking account, the most common items needed are: some type of ID, your business' EIN (which you can apply for an EIN at IRS.gov *for free*), and the Articles of Organization if it's an LLC.

The Articles of Organization are part of a legal document that establishes an LLC at the state level. It states how an LLC will operate as a business between its *members*, which is another word for the owners.

> **Side note:** You won't need a **DUNS number** when you open your business bank account. However, you will need to apply for one after you establish your business. **DUNS** is short for *Data Universal Numbering System* and can be accessed at Dun and Bradstreet (DnB.com), a company that monitors data about your business. Just like how the personal side of credit has Equifax, Experian, and TransUnion to monitor your personal credit data, Experian Business, Equifax Business, and Dun and Bradstreet are the three agencies that monitor your business credit profile. The Small Business Financial Exchange is another organization that monitors business data.

While we're talking about the legal entities, we can briefly mention some others.

This next part is also for information purposes only. Don't focus too much on this right now in the grand scheme of things. This is just a mini sidebar.

## Business Entities & LLCs

Most businesses incorporate under one of five entity types. They are:

- Sole proprietor: You can be held personally liable with this structure.
- Limited Partnership: Your liability can be limited with a partner.
- S Corporation: You can have reduced personal liability like a C Corporation, but without the double taxation. You can also have up to 100 shareholders (i.e., people who have part ownership in the company). More on shares, shareholders, and stocks later.
- C Corporation: There is Limited Liability, but *taxation* happens twice both on the business level and personal earnings level. This is one way to look at double taxation.
- Limited Liability Company (LLC): Suzie had her company setup as an LLC because she wanted her personal liability to be limited.

Although these businesses are legal entities and not tax entities, there are different tax benefits of having a legal business structure setup. When she started making more money per month within her business, she decided to have her LLC taxed as an S Corporation.

Suzie's company has grown so much that she has *licensing deals* with places such as Whole Foods and other major grocery store chains who have offered to sell her lemonade in their stores.

Now, she wants to start investing in some companies in the stock market. So, her mom sets up a custodial Roth IRA account (UTMA or UGMA) for her since she is not yet 18-years-old. UTMA stands for *Uniform Transfers to Minors Act*, and UGMA stands for *Uniform Gift to Minors Act*.

## The Quadrants in Real Life

Suzie's story could be anyone's story. The concept of how she grew her business is simple, once you understand how the pieces fit together. We'll go over other passive income ideas that are better suited for a full-time college student in just a bit.

There are other examples of how people went from one side of the quadrant to the other and generated great wealth in the process.

Ray Kroc went from the S Quadrant to the B and I Quadrants. There are also those whose names you may or may not recognize.

Here's another example of how one person overcame many of life's challenges and obstacles, and still found freedom on the right side of the quadrant.

This person worked as a salesman in the medical supply field. But he never got to the level of success he was striving for in that field. Later, things got so tough for him and his son that they ended up becoming homeless, and even found themselves sleeping on bathroom floors in subway stations.

The name of this man is Chris Gardner, and after learning about more leveraged ways to make money from a guy named Bob Bridges, he devoted everything to learn how to do it, too.

Chris Gardner was walking and saw this guy, Bob, pull up in a red Ferrari. Chris asked Bob, "What do you do? And how do you do it?" Bob later had lunch with Chris and told him how people can earn money in the stock market.

The story of Chris Gardner may be familiar to you. There was a movie made about his story starring Will Smith called *The Pursuit of Happyness* (yes, with a "Y"). The movie showed the journey of how he moved from the S Quadrant to the I Quadrant.

Now, you may think that a person can only be on the right side of the quadrant by coming from the S or self-employed quadrant. However, there are examples of people who worked a full-time job in the E quadrant, and still ended up becoming wealthy as an Investor in the I quadrant.

For the next example, meet Mr. Earl Crawley. Mr. Earl was a 69-year-old parking lot attendant in the year 2008. What was so special about Mr. Earl was that although he never made more than $12 an hour on his job, his dividend port-folio at the time was worth over half a million dollars.

On top of that, Mr. Earl was also dyslexic. Dyslexia is a learning disorder that makes processing language through speech or reading difficult. Despite any challenge Mr. Earl faced, he was still able to become financially wealthy because he learned and understood how money works.

Let's breakdown some key terms and principles that were important for Mr. Earl to understand.

# CHAPTER 10

# Investing 101

### The Eighth Wonder: A Million-Dollar Retirement Plan

Albert Einstein has been quoted often by saying, "**Compound Interest** is the Eighth Wonder of the World. He who understands it, earns it; he who doesn't, pays for it." Some say that he actually said, "Compounding numbers is the eighth wonder." Regardless, compound interest is definitely something you need to learn and understand.

**Compound interest** is when the interest a person earns on a principal balance (i.e., the original amount of money put in) is reinvested and generates additional interest or profit.

### The Rule of 72

If you want to see how long it would take for your money to double in an investment with compound interest, you can use the **Rule of 72.** If the account earns at 8%, you divide 72 by 8 and you'll get the number of years it takes for that investment to double. In this case, it would take 9 years to double. Here, 72 is divided by 8 (i.e., the interest rate) equals 9 (i.e., number of years it takes to double).

Also, keep in mind that inflation *on average* occurs at a rate of about 2% per year. **Inflation** is the rate at which the overall prices of goods and services are rising.

This is another reason that many wealthy investors prefer to have money in investments versus sitting in a savings account or under their bed mattress. Savings accounts usually have a **rate of return** of 0.06% on average in 2022. So, if you had $1,000 sitting in a savings account, you would have made a $0.60 return in that year.

## Dollar Cost Averaging

One steady and long-term investment that many people overlook, primarily because of the time period, is investing $500 a month per year from your Roth IRA into an index fund, such as the S&P 500, for 40 Years. Essentially, that will get you to $1 Million. Placing $500 a month into an investment is a strategy called **Dollar Cost Averaging**.

Now, before you ask questions like, "What's a fund?" or "What in the world is an index?" or "S & P, what?" let's backtrack a little so you can understand some basics of investing in stocks or shares.

## Stocks 101

Let's start with the basics. An **investment**, like an asset, is something that puts money into your pocket.

When you hear people talk about investing in stocks, they are really investing in or purchasing **shares** of a company. When you purchase shares of a company, you have part ownership of the company you bought the shares in.

The hope with this type of investment is that you will have some type of **capital gains. Capital gains** is when an asset increases in value over time.

There are four basic ways to invest in stocks that we will go over in this book: **individual companies, mutual funds, index funds** and **ETFs**.

## Individual Stocks

**Individual stocks**: You can invest in a single company by purchasing shares on the stock market through a broker. Again, a **broker** is like the middleman. Back in the day, you would have to purchase your stocks through an individual, or representative from a brokerage firm, who was able to purchase or sell stocks. Today, many people use online brokers because of the convenience and ease.

In the US, companies have their shares bought and sold on one of three **Exchanges**: the American Stock Exchange (**AMEX** or **ASE**), New York Stock Exchange (**NYSE**), and the National Association of Securities Dealers (**NASDAQ**).

In the earlier example, Mr. Earl's strategy was to invest in Blue Chip Stocks and have all the dividends *reinvested* back into more stock. He would take a portion of each paycheck from his job and put toward these stocks. Again, making these consistent deposits on a regular basis is called **Dollar Cost Averaging**.

**Blue Chip Stocks** are companies that are usually worth billions of dollars, pay out dividends, and are usually profitable in good and bad times long-term. Blue Chip companies are usually household names like Apple, Coca-Cola, Amazon, Nike, Verizon, Microsoft, Tesla, and Disney.

A **Dividend** is money, or a portion of the profits, paid out to the shareholders who are the people that own stock in a company.

The last thing with investing in individual stocks is that you will want to keep a close eye on each individual stock to track its performance.

The rule of thumb with stocks is that you "Buy Low, Sell High" for a profit when it's a Bull Market. Although, there are more advanced strategies that allow you to "Sell High and Buy (to cover) Low" when there is a Bear Market, also called Short Selling.

**Bull Market** is a term when stocks are moving up or expected to move up in price.

**Bear Market** is a term when there is a weak market and stocks are moving down in price.

One way to see how a stock has been doing over a certain period of time is by looking at the charts.

Have you ever seen those squiggly lines that look like mountain peaks and valleys? They show how well or how bad a stock has been performing over a set time period.

You can adjust the time periods of those charts to show you Year to Date (YTD), 52 weeks (i.e., over the last year), six months, three months, and all the way down to weekly and daily charts.

The top of the mountain peaks, also called *resistance level*, will be the highest price point that a stock was bought and sold at. And the valleys, also called *support level*, will show you the lowest price point bought and sold.

**Side note**: There are more advanced charts that may show these "mountain peak" lines that have rectangle shapes on them. These are **candlestick charts** that mostly day traders use to give more detailed information on how that stock is performing.

## *Mutual Funds*

Next, we have **Mutual Funds**. Mutual Funds are funds where many investors pool their money together and invest in diversified investments.

**Diversification** is a strategy to reduce risks by a mix or different types of investments. Mutual Funds are usually a combination of stocks, bonds, and sometimes commodities.

A **Bond** is money you lend to a corporation or government that is paid back in full after a certain time period. While you hold the bond, you are often paid interest on that amount you loaned.

**Commodities** are raw materials or basic goods that are interchangeable with other goods. There are three types—agriculture, energy, and metals. There are commodities such as gold, coal, oil, corn, and sugar.

The only reason I prefer Index Funds over Mutual Funds at this stage is that the fund is managed by a "fund manager" and the fees are often higher. However, if you did want an advisor with little to no fees help you reach certain financial goals within a certain time period, you can do your research on companies that have robo-advisor services such as SoFi.com or Betterment.com, which will adjust your investments based on your goals.

## *Index Funds*

**Index Funds** are a type of mutual fund where the investments follow or track a market index. The index is usually based on a formula of some sort. For simplicity's sake, this formula could mean if these stocks meet these criteria, they'll fall in this index.

One of the more popular indexes (or indices if you want to sound fancy) is the Standard & Poor's 500, also called the S&P 500. This an index of the Top 500 companies in the US. This index fund purchases shares from each of the companies listed. So, if you invested in the S&P 500, 6% of the money invested might go toward Amazon, while 0.6% might go toward Nike.

Instead of investing in each of those 500 individual stocks, investing in that one index fund would essentially do the same thing. As discussed before, you could put money into your Roth IRA and then invest in the S&P 500, which by the way has averaged over a 10% return over the past two decades according to spglobal.com.

People can also invest in certain sectors like the Tech or Oil Sectors, for example.

## *ETFs*

**ETFs (Exchange Traded Funds)** are very similar to index funds. You can invest in an ETF like you invest in a stock. The main difference is that you can buy and sell an ETF throughout the day when and if the price changes. Index funds can only be bought and sold once a day when the market closes at 4:00 pm (Eastern Standard Time).

Because the overall strategy mentioned in this book is long-term and more passive, we will focus on index funds for now. As you learn more and become more advanced, you can be more active and hands-on with your investing.

## *Cryptocurrency*

**Cryptocurrency** is a digital currency or money that uses cryptography to make secure payments from one person to the next anywhere around the world.

This cryptography that keeps things secured or *verified* is known as the blockchain. The **Blockchain** is a digital ledger that is verified by thousands of computers all around the world. **Bitcoin** was the first of its kind when it was created in 2008. Experts say that Bitcoin will one day reach $1 million, while billionaire investor Warren Buffett said he wouldn't buy Bitcoin because he believes it doesn't produce anything tangible.

There are people who have invested in Bitcoin, cryptocurrencies, and other digital assets like Altcoins, Non-Fungible Tokens (NFTs), and more to gain profit. Some even do things like Crypto Currency Mining, while others participate in things called Uniswap liquidity pools on sites such as Zapper.fi. But for this stage in the game, I would learn the ins and outs before actively investing.

The main difference between the US banking system and cryptocurrency is that the US banking system is centralized, where cryptocurrency is decentralized.

# CHAPTER 11

# Passive Income

*"*Here's Economics 101. Person A gives **Value** to Person B. Person B then gives money to Person A in exchange for that value." –Frank Kern

Now, for the book section you've *probably* been waiting on. The reason this portion is the last section of the book is because you needed to understand the foundation of all the steps *before* learning how to properly build passive income as a college student.

Meaning, everything from learning patience and doing the right activities over a period of time through the scholarship application process, to the daily habits of how to budget and allocate your money. Each framework has its proper place.

Just like you wouldn't expect to be awarded a scholarship the second you submit the application, you should have a financial mindset of patience and doing the right activities over time.

The first milestone I want you to reach is to make your first dollar in your sleep (i.e., or money you didn't actively do something to receive). Next, I want you to get to the point where you generate enough passively to cover your tuition and fees for one semester. After that, have enough to cover tuition and fees, and all *other* expenses you have for the semester such as: room and board or housing, meals, and textbooks. Lastly, set a goal to have more than enough coming in passively to cover a full academic year.

The key thing to remember is that it will be a gradual process. Keep that in mind, and you will be on your way.

## *Passive Income Explained*

So, what is Passive Income? **Passive income** is income or money that can be earned automatically without any or minimal effort from you. In other words, passive income can be defined as *money you make in your sleep*.

As we mentioned before when talking about the business owner quadrant, you can work or pay someone to set up a system one time, and have that system pay you over and over again.

There are hundreds, if not thousands, of ways to generate passive income streams. But the only ones we'll outline in this section will allow you to focus on your academics, and not *in* the business.

The key here is to first generate enough money to cover your educational costs that aren't fully covered by scholarships. Don't get me wrong. The goal *is* to have more than enough in scholarships to cover everything. But, in the case you do *not* receive enough in scholarships, this is a backup strategy to not only cover that cost but put money in your pocket, too.

Before we go into the different passive income streams, we need to lay some foundational principles.

First, we need to understand that these concepts are not get rich quick schemes. They are passive income streams. Please understand that there is some initial up-front *work* that needs to be done to properly set up your systems to generate that passive income.

Next, we need to understand the "Riches are in the Niches" strategy. Some pronounce it "Neeshes," but that doesn't rhyme anymore, does it?

Anyway, I bet you're wondering what any of that means, huh?

## Riches in the Niches

A **niche** is defined as a market segment for a certain type of product or service. What are you naturally good at? What do people come to seek your advice or expertise in?

Instead of focusing on any random idea that comes across your head or social media timeline, list out on a sheet of paper all the things you are either knowledgeable of, skilled at, or interests you.

After you list them all out, we will pick the niche or category that you are the most knowledgeable of and interests you the most. The "Big Three" areas that I recommend your profit stream(s) focus on are either: Health, Wealth, or Relationships.

Once we figure out which major niche your category falls under, we will go down one more level into what's called the sub-niche level. For example, if your area falls under the Health category, a sub-niche could be Fitness.

We would then go one more level down, and your area of focus could be "Female Fitness for College Students" for example. With this idea, you or your products and services can be the go-to for people in that sub-niche. Instead of being a small fish in a big pond, you can be the big fish in a smaller pond.

Click Funnels co-founder and author, Russell Brunson, describes the Big Three niche level as a "Red Ocean." Things are too competitive on that level now. But when you "niche-down" a couple levels, then you start to stand out in your own "Blue Ocean" where things are not as competitive for what you are offering.

## Money in the List

The next foundational principle to understand is that the "Money is in the List" or the "Fortunes are in the Follow-up."

What does that even mean?

For starters, the people who end up buying your passive income stream products and services are on a journey between where they are now with some sort of problem and finding the solution with what you have to offer.

The truth is most people will not buy on the first exposure to what you're offering. On top of that, they may never see that offer again if you don't have a way of systematically following up with that prospective customer.

Most people are bombarded with so many advertisements and marketing messages all day. As soon as they see an offer, especially one that doesn't speak to their current problem or pain, they've forgotten about it instantly.

But what if they are somewhat interested, but not at a time or place where they can purchase right then?

This is where the "Money in the List" term comes into play. The **list** refers to having a list of prospective customers with their basic contact information for the purpose of following up with them. Most times, this can be as simple as a name and email address.

But how do we get their names and contact information? This process is known as **Direct Response Marketing**. This is a marketing strategy with the intent to get an immediate or *direct* response from your prospective customers to take a specific action.

Why would they want to give you their contact information? They will gladly give their name and email to you because you are going to give them something of value in exchange for it.

Most people will be looking for a solution, a strategy, a discount, or an answer to their current problem. If you can provide something that can either solve it or get them one step closer to what they are looking for, they will give you their information. When you lead with value or results in advance, they will reciprocate with the email, which is what's called the **call to action**.

I like how Joe Polish and Dean Jackson from ILoveMarketing.com put it. They say, "You want your prospective customer to figuratively raise their hand."

## The Three C's Explained

### Create, Capture, & Convert

This last foundational principle that you must understand is knowing the three steps your passive income system needs to be successful.

I like how entrepreneur, Chris Record, breaks down the three parts of the system. They are: Create Traffic, Capture Leads, and Convert Sales.

### Create Traffic

Yes, it says "Create" traffic. But we're not really creating the traffic. What we're doing is placing our offer where the traffic already is. This can be on Instagram, Facebook (Meta) Groups, Twitter, Niched Forums, or Blogs. By **traffic**, I mean people or online visitors who are interested in the subject of what you have to offer.

There are essentially two types of ways to generate traffic for your offer: Organic Traffic and Paid Traffic.

**Organic Traffic** is when you have built up a following of interested followers on any online platform, or targeted people searching for your solution based on keywords and other factors that will lead them "organically" to you over time.

There are pros and cons to getting organic traffic to your offer.

**Pros**: It is free to get organic traffic, and just takes some time on your part.

**Cons**: The traffic is unpredictable and takes time on your part to generate enough traffic to meet your sales goals.

**Paid Traffic** is when you can pay someone or a platform—such as Facebook (Meta) or Instagram, Snapchat Ads Platform—to place your ads or offer to a certain audience group for a certain period.

**Pros:** You can often get detailed information about how much the cost per click (CPC), cost per lead (CPL), or cost per acquisition (CPA) is, down to the penny.

**Side note**: This is mostly when using the official advertising part of those platforms. This is a separate strategy from messaging an influencer with a lot of followers in your niche on Instagram and asking him or her to promote a product or post to their followers.

**Cons**: It costs money to use this strategy. And if you do not know what you are doing or don't use a professional to run your ads for you, then you could end up spending more money than necessary to get traffic.

## Capture Leads

The next part is to **Capture Leads**. We already discussed the overall strategy.

The only thing I want to add is that you need to have some type of software to capture the leads, and *automatically* send about five to seven emails to follow up with that prospective customer about your original offer. This software is known as an **email autoresponder**. And the emails will be sent automatically each day after they enter their email address for however many messages you want to send.

There are plenty of free autoresponders out there up to a certain number of **subscribers** (i.e., the people or leads who enter their email), as well as paid ones that are more sophisticated.

Currently, some of the email autoresponders include: SendinBlue, MailerLite, Sender, Aweber, Moosend, and ConvertKit.

For now, you'll probably want to stick to the free ones until you start getting enough passive income to pay for the ones that have a few more bells and whistles to better automate the process.

## Convert Sales

The process of converting those leads or prospective customers into actual paying customers is mostly in the automatic follow-up communication.

There are other ways of following up via tracking pixels and other advanced strategies that we won't explore in this book. Essentially, the way to increase the likelihood of someone purchasing one of your Passive Income Stream products is by placing it in front of them enough until the time is right for them.

**Three Ways to Generate More Revenue**

Once they buy from you, there are three ways that you can increase the amount of passive income you'll receive in the long term.

Entrepreneur and Business Coach, Jay Abraham, says the three ways to grow your business is to either:

1. Increase the number of customers
2. Increase the average transaction value (i.e., how much spent at one time)
3. Increase purchasing frequency (repeat buyers)

I like how Entrepreneur and Businesswoman, Richelle Shaw, also says it:

1. How am I going to get customers?
2. How am I going to get them more often?
3. How am I going to get them to *expand* the transaction to buy more every time they buy from me?

Whew! Breathe! If any of those concepts are brand new to you, don't worry. It will make more and more sense over time. You may think that none of that information was necessary. But please believe me when I say that if I understood those concepts when I first started to build passive income streams, it would have saved me a lot of time, money, and headaches.

## *15 Passive Income Streams for College Students*

In this next part, I will list out different passive income streams that you can use to generate money for your educational costs first, and *then* to your different accounts that we went over in section two earlier.

They are in no specific order. Meaning, the first one isn't necessarily the best one for you. Review all of them, and then decide which one would work best.

### Passive Income Stream #1: Start a Podcast

A **Podcast** is a series of audio files that people can listen to or download from the internet. They are also available on popular platforms such as Apple Podcasts, Spotify, Buzzsprout, and Captivate.

You can simply take out your phone, hit record, and start talking. Okay, I know that's a *major* simplification of setting up a podcast. And there's a little bit more to it than that. But after you get the content out there and you start getting better over time, you will start to build an audience that resonates with you.

According to the creative content marketing agency Brafton.com, there are basically eight different types of podcasts:

1. Interview podcasts: you and possibly another host interview people.
2. Conversational podcasts: two hosts talk about various themes and topics.
3. Monologue podcasts: you talk solo about a specific subject.
4. Storytelling podcasts: you tell a story or part of one in each episode.
5. Roundtable podcasts: a group of hosts have conversations on topics.
6. Theatrical podcasts: you narrate a story or an entire cast performs.
7. Repurposed content podcasts: you reiterate a story from another medium, like a blog, video, etc.
8. Hybrid podcasts: you mix or combine different type of podcasts.

**Monetizing Your Podcast**

One of the more popular ways that people monetize podcasts is by securing sponsors and advertisements.

Have you ever heard a podcast, and then somewhere in the beginning, middle or end you hear something like, "This episode was brought to you by..."? More times than not, someone paid the host of that podcast to give their business or brand a shout out. In addition, they usually have some type of *call to action* so the audience can follow up to find more information.

> **Side note**: Some of the more popular ad networks that find brands who might want to advertise on your podcasts include Midroll, as well as Authentic, for example.

Another way podcasters monetize is by promoting their own products or services on the show.

My recommendation is to video record your podcasts with the intent to *repurpose* the episode for another use. Repurposing the content means that you can take the content and upload it on another platform or medium such as YouTube for example.

Even if you don't have a camera, you can record Zoom interviews, for example and extract the audio for your podcast. Zoom is a video conferencing platform used for virtual meetings, events, phone calls, and webinars among other things.

Two people who really breakdown how to start a podcast from scratch and scale it in a profitable way are: Pat Flynn from SmartPassiveIncome.com and David Shands from the Social Proof Podcast.

**Passive Income Stream #2: Starting a YouTube Channel**

Let's say that you decide to repurpose your podcast video content and upload it on your brand-new YouTube channel that is niche-specific to your topic. You can start building your audience on that platform as well.

The passive ways to monetize your YouTube channel is first by **AdSense**. YouTube AdSense is where businesses can purchase ad space and YouTube can place their ads on videos that are mostly related to that video ad.

Currently, for your YouTube channel or account to be eligible for AdSense, your channel would need a total of 4,000 hours of your videos watched and at least 1,000 subscribers.

At first, the amounts you get paid will be smaller amounts. But as your channel, subscribers, and views increase, you should start to see the passive income you receive grow.

**Passive Income Stream #3: Digital Products**

A **digital product** is a product that can be sold online, and the buyer gets online access to that product via instant download or via email.

Some examples of digital products can include:

- Digital planners
- Checklists
- Calendars
- Recipe PDFs

You can use resources like **Canva.com** and **BookBolt.io** to create and modify design templates for many digital products.

Your next step is to place your newly created digital product on sites like Etsy or Amazon. If you are continuing to provide value to your niche audience, then your digital products should be centered around solving a problem they have. You could even go a step further and demonstrate on a "YouTube Video Walkthrough" of how it will help them. Then, your call to action could be telling your viewers to "click the link in the description" to get access to it.

**Passive Income Stream #4: eBooks & Low-Content Books**

After digital products, the eBooks and low-content books are an easy transition. The main reason is because you can use the digital version of items such as journals, planners, and even children's coloring books, and have platforms create and sell the *physical* version of them *for you*.

For example, you could take a journal you've created in digital format and upload it to a platform called **Amazon KDP**, which stands for Kindle Direct Publishing.

You simply upload the digital version with the correct specifications, and then it's ready for people to buy it directly from Amazon. If you need help or ideas for content for your low-content book, you can go to sites like **KDPinterior.com** for free and inexpensive templates that you can modify and sell.

Or perhaps you want someone else to write a book for you completely from scratch that you will have full ownership of and rights to sell. This strategy is known as using a ghostwriter service. There are ghostwriting sites like TheUrbanWriters.com, GhostBookWriters.org, and EliteAuthors.com to name a few.

Or maybe you want to sell a book that's already written and want to have the rights to sell it as your own. This is what is known as **Private Label Rights**. You can find PLR Books at sites like IDPLR.com for example.

**Passive Income Stream #5: Affiliate Marketing**

Have you ever recommended a great restaurant, movie, or even something as simple as the most comfortable pair of shoes you've ever worn? I'm pretty sure you have. What if every time you referred someone to one of those things that company paid you for sending them? That, my friend, is considered **Affiliate Marketing**.

Affiliate marketing is when you are the middle person between a product and potential customers, and you receive a commission for that referral.

There are so many affiliate programs and networks out there that people don't know about. For example, places like Walmart, Target, Home Depot, and Old Navy have affiliate programs. The easiest way to find them is to do a search by typing the company name followed by "affiliate program."

Once you get signed up with your personal information and where you want them to send the **commissions** (i.e., the money earned for the referrals), they will give you a unique web address that will tie all the sales back to you. Those commissions may not have a high percentage though.

For products that have more volume, traffic, or a higher percentage of commission payouts, there are sites like:

Refersion (geared toward eCommerce sites), CJ.com (formerly Commission Junction), Amazon Associates (for products sold on Amazon), ClickBank.com (for digital products and courses), and several others.

The percentage of commission you'll earn varies from platform to platform. For example, you may receive 5%-6% commission on a product you refer from Amazon, while you could potentially earn a 50%-70% commission for a digital course sold on the ClickBank Marketplace.

**Quick Tip**: Higher ticket products yield higher commissions.

Once you have your niche determined, you can refer your followers to products that will help them find solutions to their problems. One way to do some quick and easy **market research** and see what's currently selling is to go on a platform like TikTok or Instagram and do a search for #AmazonFinds or #TikTokMadeMeBuyIt for example. This search will result in the most popular and trending products out right now.

If using YouTube, you could place a link to a **bridge page** in your description that recaps or further describes the product. A bridge page can be considered the webpage that "bridges" the connection between your affiliate link and the sales page of the product you're promoting. Marketers use this method to increase the **conversions** (i.e., another word for the percentage of people who take a certain action, and in this case buy the product). So, if 3 out of 100 people that clicked your affiliate link end up buying that product, then that would be a 3% conversion. Many of the email autoresponder platforms mentioned earlier allow you to easily create bridge pages or landing pages to collect emails. I used to miss out on so many sales because I didn't create a landing page to collect emails for follow up, nor did I have a bridge page to increase conversions. I would still make those daily commissions, but just imagine how much more I could have earned had I done that simple extra step.

**Side note**: Be sure to use a URL shortener like Bitly.com or Tinyurl.com to shorten your link to your bridge page. Another step that you could take in promoting your offer on Instagram or TikTok is to go to Linktr.ee and set up a LinkTree for the different products you are promoting. That way, you can simply say "click on the link in the bio" for more information. That one link will give access to a "Tree of Links" that your viewers can see.

## Passive Income Stream #6: Courses

When it comes to creating and selling courses online, there is a right way and a wrong way to do it. This income stream is also a real way to generate passive and leveraged income for yourself. Entrepreneurs and course creators like Ashley Grayson (the former Ashley Massengill) are prime examples of how people can literally start from nothing and create a dream lifestyle for themselves and family by creating massive amounts of value for others through courses and coaching. Or others like Dan Henry, founder of GetClients.com and author of "Digital

Millionaire Secrets," has a unique way of validating and preselling a course before it's even created.

When creating an online course, one way to find out what the people in that niche want to learn is simply by asking them, "What do you want to know?" You could ask in the form of a social media post, survey, a niched Facebook group, or Google form. Just be sure to keep it simple. You can say something like, "What is your biggest challenge regarding (your subject or course idea)?" Then, after you get around one hundred responses, you can rank the ideas based on those responses. After you get about six to eight of the top responses, you now have a framework that you can work from. These six to eight topics could be the modules for your online course, and you can teach them what, why, and how to do whatever it is your teaching them to "get them the result."

That is the key part. They are looking for a specific result by the time they get to the end of your course. The way you do your lessons can vary. You can record your voice over presentation slides, you can talk to the camera, or you could even interview someone who is an expert in that area you are covering in that module.

After you are done recording, you can then upload the content on online course platforms such as Teachable or Skillshare. ClickFunnels or Kajabi can give you a little more customization and tools as your online course business grows.

## Passive Income Stream #7: Membership Sites & Paid Subscriptions

Membership sites or paid subscription services are a business model that allow you to create content in the form of videos, audios, and newsletters. Your followers can pay you on a monthly or annual basis to have access to your content. There are two main differences between an online course and a membership site. One difference is that the membership site content will always be new and shared with your audience on a regular basis. Some release new content to their paying subscribers once a week or even once a month, as long as the value exceeds the cost of the membership. You want to provide at least 10 times the amount of value over the membership cost. Therefore, if the cost is $100 a month per subscriber, then you should be providing at least $1,000 worth of content in value.

The second difference is that the subscribers will pay you on an ongoing basis, until they decide to cancel their membership.

Sites like Patreon.com and Fanbase.com were created specifically for businesses like this. Both, Patreon and Fanbase allow you to give exclusive content and access to a community, while developing a recurring income stream.

## Passive Income Stream #8: Print On Demand (POD)

**Print On Demand** is when you can have clothing or other items with your logo or designs on them, printed and shipped to the customer without having to hold inventory. You can have everything from t-shirts, cups and mugs, blankets, socks, to almost anything else you can think of. The great part about this income stream is that you don't have to do anything but add the design, and the POD company takes care of the fulfillment for you.

**Teespring.com** or **Printify.com** are just a couple of sites where you can sell these types of products. You can also embed the product links in your content descriptions of your other passive income streams.

**RedBubble.com** is a site with constant traffic that you can upload your digital art to be placed on different types of products.

For designs and other types of freelance work, you could pay someone to create it for you on sites like Fiverr.com or Upwork.com. You can also purchase design bundles on sites like CreativeFabrica.com

**Passive Income Stream #9: *Owning* A Business**

Going back to the Cashflow Quadrant ™, one of my students was interested in learning graphic design and creating a business out of it. He initially worked from the self-employed quadrant. Every time an organization on campus wanted a flyer for their event or party, he charged them $30 for the flyer. He started making money almost instantly because his service was in high demand on campus. After going over the Cashflow Quadrant ™ with him, he wanted to know how he could turn his graphic design business from the S quadrant to the B quadrant.

Here's what we came up with. I asked him, "You're currently charging $30 per flyer that you make, right?" He said, "Yes." So, essentially the plan was to hire other graphic designers on campus looking for work or find graphic designers on Fiverr.com who charge less than $20 per flyer to make the flyers for his company. He would get the flyer requests via messages on his business Instagram page and assign the jobs to the other graphic designers. Once they do the job to the specifications, he would pay them $20, and he would keep $10 just for owning the business. His next plan is for someone to run the business for him at a set price, and he keeps $10 for each flyer made without having to do any active work.

Another business idea could be to start with a product that you had custom made or manufactured to sell on your own eCommerce store, which can be created at Shopify.com.

**Side note**: Your Shopify store may take some more upfront time to get setup. An alternative that allows you to place up to five products for free is a site called BigCartel.com. The setup is much easier and faster, especially with POD products. Another alternative to Shopify could be using a platform like Zyro.com, which allows you to build a website with a simple, point, click and drag.

For example, take somebody like Chris Winter. He combined two of the passive income streams by taking his POD shirts centered around Entrepreneurship and created an entire business and eCommerce store called Entrepreneurshirts.co. He can then choose to run the store himself or have someone run it for him as he keeps earning passive income.

**Passive Income Stream #10: Develop Software (SAAS) or an App**

SAAS stands for Software As A Service. The key thing to understand is this is software that a business or consumer would pay each month or year to have access to. It would be setup like the electric company charging people each month for access to electricity.

Years ago, I wouldn't have even considered listing this as one of the passive income streams. But after I heard the Smart Passive Income Podcast episode 46 where Pat Flynn interviewed the author of *Start From Zero*, Dane Maxwell, on how to start a software company from scratch, I realized that you didn't have to know code or be a software designer to do so.

As a matter of fact, he didn't know how to do any of that stuff. Yet, he built million-dollar software companies. He was able to validate the idea of the software as a service before the creation process even began. He says when coming up with the idea during a process called idea extraction. He says, "When you can define their problem better than they can, they automatically assume you have the solution."

Essentially, he asks about 100 or more people in any industry what their biggest problems or challenges are regarding the time wasters or obstacles to getting more sales. He also asks them if they had a magic button or software that would make everything perfect, what would it do and how would it look? Next, the key thing is to ask them how much they would pay monthly for a software like this. Once he gets your average, he can grandfather them into the first year or lifetime for a set price. That set price could be the cost to get it developed.

Then, he would find someone who specializes in UI (i.e., User Interface or the look of the software) on a site like Upwork.com and ask what their rate would be to mockup the design. He gets a simple working model with those designs and goes back to those original 100 and ask what they like, dislike, or what changes would they make.

After he gets all the updates and changes, he then pays for and sends the design (UI) to a coder to "code it out" to the specifications to create an MVP (Minimum Viable Product). Now, he owns the software outright and can charge monthly for access to it.

Then, he can hire a manager or CEO to run the company for him and get a 50/50 split of all gross profit.

**Passive Income Stream #11: Blog**

**Blogging** can be considered your very own online magazine where people read your content.

You can setup a free blog on sites like Wix, WordPress, Blogger, or Medium.

**SaveTheStudent.org** is a popular blogging platform where students already congregate with the mindset to read on various topics. The advantage here is that you can position yourself to provide the best content regarding your niche—if related to student topics in this example. Let's say that you don't know what to write about or don't feel like typing out the blog. You could use an online transcription service like **Otter.ai** to have your voice or video recording transcribed.

There are several ways to monetize your blog. You can post affiliate links within your blog post, place banner advertisements on your blog that people pay you to place, sell your digital products or physical products on there, or you can do product reviews for a set price.

**Passive Income Stream #12: Social Media Promotions (IG)**

This passive income stream works really well once you have built your following to a significant number. Since the Instagram (IG) profile you have set up for your niche is targeted, people within that niche will more than likely message and want to pay you to promote their product in some way.

One way is by making a post on your IG account. You can mention it in a video, or you could promote it within a 24-hour period in your Instagram Stories.

## Passive Income Stream #13: Selling Stock Photos & Video

There are content creators, businesses, and other influencers who are always looking for great photos, videos, or drone footage that they can integrate in their marketing messages.

**Foap.com** is a website where you can get paid repeatedly for your photos or videos that can be used by others.

**Shutterstock.com** or **MotionArray.com** are a sites you can use once you get more comfortable and your images and videos look more professional.

One key tip is to focus your photos and videos on certain trends, popular locations, events, and holidays.

## Passive Income Stream #14: Put Ads on Your Car

When you go off to school, you may be in a highly populated area where there are tons of businesses. Sometimes, these businesses have an advertising budget that they can use to help get their name out to the local community.

There are some businesses that will pay you monthly to advertise their business on your car. **Wrapify.com** is a service that does just that. You can download the app from the app store to see if your vehicle is eligible to participate. They will wrap your car with the company's ad, and when you are finished with your advertising campaign the wrap comes off clean.

**Passive Income Stream #15: Sell Your Class Notes**

Sometimes, there are emergencies that come up when a student cannot attend class in person. Although the reading assignment may be given, there are times when the notes from the in-person lecture helps a student better understand the reading material.

Did you know that there are platforms where you can post your notes from class *and* get paid for it? Yes, there are sites like **NexusNotes.com** that will allow you to post notes on various subjects to earn some passive income. Another similar platform is **StuDocu.com**.

**Recap – Grow the Money**

In this section, you learned why the wealthy buy assets instead of liabilities, and how those assets fund their lifestyle. You also learned about the four ways to generate income. We went over different types of investments and investment strategies, and listed 15 different passive income streams that are ideal for college students.

# CONCLUSION

**Y**ou made it! First, I want to say congratulations for completing this book. Also, I want to thank you for going on this financial literacy journey with me. I hope this book has given you the tools, resources, and most importantly, the confidence in yourself to better understand your relationship with money and improving your financial IQ. You will be able to use the principles outlined in this book for years and years to come. The key thing is to take it one step at a time, one day at a time, and soon you'll be able to see how far you've come.

If you picked up anything from this book worthwhile, please do me a *huge* favor and do two things:

First, head over to Amazon and leave a review of how this book made an impact on you.

After that, head over to https://FinLitUniversity.net/review and leave me a testimonial. Thank you so much in advance for doing that for me! It really means a lot.

# REFERENCES

Abraham, J. (2001). Getting everything you can out of all you've got: 21 ways you can out-think, out-perform, and out-earn the competition (1st ed.). St. Martin's Griffin Publishing.

Aliche, T. (2021). Get good with money : ten simple steps to becoming financially whole. New York: Harmony Books.

Black, M. & Adams, D. (2022, June 15). *Does Being An Authorized User Build Credit?* Forbes. https://www.forbes.com/advisor/credit-cards/will-being-an-authorized-user-help-you-build-  credit/

Crowe, C. (1996). Jerry Maguire. "Show me the money!" Line spoken by Rod Tidwell, played by Cuba Gooding, Jr., TriStar Pictures.

Curtis, R. (2021). Mastering your money mindset: self discovery book. Be Boujee Enterprises, LLC.

Gardner, C. (2006). The pursuit of happyness. HarperCollins Publishers.

Gray, C. (2021). Go where there is no path: stories of hustle, grit, scholarship, and faith. HarperCollins Publishers.

Hanson, M. "Student loan debt statistics" EducationData.org, May 30, 2022,https://educationdata.org/student-loan-debt-statistics

Kavilanz, P. (2016, February 29). *How one high schooler made $80K (without getting a job)*. CNN. https://money.cnn.com/2015/09/18/smallbusiness/raiseme-college-scholarship/

Kiyosaki, R. T. (2017). Rich dad poor dad (2nd ed.). Plata Publishing.

Merriam-Webster. (2003). Merriam-Webster's collegiate dictionary (11th ed.).

Michalowicz, M. (2017). Profit first : transform your business from a cash-eating monster to a money-making machine . New York: Portfolio Penguin.

Shaw, R. (2012). The million dollar equation: how to build a million dollar business in 3 years or less. Createspace Independent Pub.

# RESOURCES

For a list of the resources mentioned in this book, please go to: FinLitUniversity.net/resources

For permission requests, speaking inquiries, and bulk order purchase options, email info@finlituniversity.net

**Work with Mr. C and his team**

We have a coaching program with limited spots available that walks students, and often parents too, though the steps and principles outlined in this book to help them create a step-by-step plan to graduate debt free. If you would like to know more about this program and see if you qualify, go to the website listed to apply and schedule a call. The website is :

https://FinLitUniversity.net/apply

**Connect with Mr. C:**

@theFinLitGuy          @theFinLitGuy

# ABOUT THE AUTHOR

Chris "Mr. C" Corinthian has worked for over 15 years in higher education in the areas of financial aid and financial literacy. After working with thousands of students, he realized that there were certain repeatable steps that students did to receive multiple scholarships and graduate debt-free. Unfortunately, there were also students who did not know this information and dropped out of school because they did not have enough money to complete college.

The United States has over $1.7 trillion in student loan debt. Chris is on a mission to stop that number from rising by showing students the blueprint to not only graduate debt-free, but also show them how they can have money in the bank when they walk across that stage at graduation. To date, he has helped students generate over six figures in scholarship awards.

Through teaching the principles of financial literacy, he walks high school seniors and current college students through a three-step framework on how to "find the money, budget the money, and grow the money" to pay for school. This book will take you on the journey of learning the foundational principles on money, and how it relates to you as a current or prospective college student.